D0066008

A HISTORY OF BRITAIN

BOOK IV

This fourth volume of the evolving series covers the Stuart period (1603-1714), opening with the would-be terrorism of the Gunpowder Plot, and leading on to the protracted struggle between King and Parliament and the Civil War. King Charles Ist lost his head in 1649 and Oliver Cromwell assumed power, yet only after the monarchy's Restoration and the 'Glorious Revolution' of 1688 was a unified British Isles set to expand the country's authority through its companies of merchant adventurers, Marlborough's victories against France, and its architects (like Wren) and scientists (like Newton) heralding the Enlightenment.

EH Carter was Chief Inspector of Schools in the 1930s and '40s.
RAF Mears taught history at Warwick School between 1923 and 1933.

David Evans, who edits the restored series, is an historian and former Head of History at Eton College.

PUBLICATION SCHEDULE

A HISTORY OF BRITAIN

BOOK IV

The Stuarts, Cromwell
and the Glorious Revolution ♦ 1603–1714

by

EH Carter & RAF Mears

edited and updated by

David Evans

STACEY
INTERNATIONAL

A History of Britain
Book IV

STACEY INTERNATIONAL
128 Kensington Church Street
London W8 4BH
Tel: +44 (0)20 7221 7166; Fax: +44 (0)20 7792 9288
Email: info@stacey-international.co.uk
www.stacey-international.co.uk

ISBN: 978 1906768 23 2

This edition © Stacey International 2010
Reprinted 2010

Original edition published in 1937 by The Clarendon Press

3 5 7 9 0 8 6 4 2

Printed in the UAE

The Publishers of this edition of *The History of Britain*, revised by David Evans (formerly Head of History, Eton College), give wholehearted acknowledgment to the original work of the late E H Carter (sometime Chief Examiner in History, Board of Education, and H M Inspector of Schools) and R A F Mears (former Senior History Master, Warwick School), who died respectively in 1954 and 1940. The Publishers declare that prolonged endeavours devoted to tracing whether rights to the work of these two distinguished scholars rested with any successors or assigns have been without avail, and that they remain ready to indemnify, as may be mutually deemed appropriate, proven holders of such rights.

Cover image courtesy of FCIT
Maps by Amber Sheers

CIP Data: A catalogue record for this book is available from the British Library

Contents

List of Illustrations

List of Maps

OUTLINE SUMMARY

EARLY STUART PERIOD (1603-60)

BRITISH ISLES   ABROAD
1603 James VI (Scotland) – James I (England)
1605 Gunpowder Plot

                                           1607 Virginia founded
1616 Shakespeare *d*.

                                           1620 Pilgrim Fathers
1642-8 Civil War   1643-1715 Louis XIV (France)
1649-53 Commonwealth   1652-4 First Dutch War
1653-8 Oliver Cromwell Protector   1655 English take Jamaica
1660 Restoration of Charles II

LATER STUART PERIOD (1660-88)

1660-85 Charles II
                                           1664 English take New York
1665-6 Plague and Fire of London
1678-80 Popish Plot
1685 Monmouth's Rebellion
1688 The Revolution

WILLIAM AND MARY, AND ANNE (1688-1714)

1689 William and Mary *acc*.
1702-14 Anne   1702-13 War of Spanish Succession

                                           1704 ⚔ Blenheim
                                           1704 English take Gibraltar
1707 Union of England and Scotland

                                           1713 Treaty of Utrecht

THE SEVENTEENTH CENTURY: INTRODUCTION

WHEN the seventeenth century began, the great revival of Catholicism, which had been proceeding since the mid-sixteenth century, had yet to reach its high point. In the Netherlands, the Spaniards consolidated the hold of Catholicism in the south (modern Belgium) and made a fresh attempt to bring the Dutch back under their religious and political control. In France, the Protestants were stripped of their privileges in the 1620s, though they preserved their freedom of worship till 1685. In the Empire the Catholic Habsburg Emperor was challenged by the Calvinist Elector Palatine, but the Emperor defeated this enemy and seized his opportunity in the first stages of the Thirty Years War (1618-1648) greatly to improve the position of Catholicism in Germany. Habsburg successes, however, alarmed neighbouring powers, including France, which, though Catholic, feared Habsburg power. The Thirty Years War finally turned into a war between France and the Habsburgs of Austria and Spain. When peace at last came to Europe in 1659, the power of Spain had been broken and France had replaced it as the premier power in Europe.

By the middle of the century, the Dutch, who had finally been recognized as independent by Spain, were the greatest trading power in Europe, with Amsterdam as the most important European port. They had acquired a large colonial empire centred on the East Indies (modern Indonesia). Their success aroused the intense jealousy of their rivals such as France and England. France was the greatest military power. Its armies were the largest, best organized and most expertly led in Europe. The main themes of western European affairs in the later 17th century were the attempts of France under King Louis XIV to extend its borders and power and the efforts of the other European powers such as the Dutch and the Habsburgs to prevent it from doing so.

France, the most successful state in Europe, seemed to owe its success to the royal absolutism which had developed in the course of the century. King Louis XIII (1610-43) and King Louis XIV (1643-1715) threw off most limitations on their power, developed a more effective bureaucracy and hugely increased the size of their standing army. These things could be funded only by an enormous increase in the burden of taxation levied on the country. The taxes paid too for Louis XIV's vast new palace at Versailles, by means of which he fascinated both his own subjects and the other European powers. Versailles became the model for courts throughout Europe, just as other rulers began to imitate Louis' system of government. Parliamentary bodies usually acted to protect the taxpayers from royal financial demands. From the ruler's point of view, they prevented him from securing what he needed to look after the interests of the state. Rulers therefore acted to remove or reduce the powers of such bodies.

Like other European rulers, the 17th century Kings of England wanted to play a significant role in foreign affairs, all the more so now that they could boast of imperial status as Kings of three kingdoms. Some of their subjects expected that their Kings might champion the Protestant cause against the Habsburgs in the early part of the century and against Catholic France later on. Yet the Stuart Kings were not well equipped to intervene in Europe. The antiquated financial system which they inherited from the Tudors was not fit for the purpose, but Parliament stood in the way of reform. In retrospect, Elizabeth seemed to have succeeded against her enemies by means of a cheap, even profitable, war at sea. Her lack of maritime success in the 1590s was forgotten and a complete lack of realism about the likely costs of any war prevailed. Given this background, the relationship between the Stuart Kings and their Parliaments was likely to prove deeply frustrating to both sides and the country was unlikely to count for much in European affairs. It is not surprising that the only time before 1688 when Britain acted as a major power was during the 1650s, when the country was under military rule and the power of the Parliaments that Cromwell summoned was weak.

The Stuart Kings also inherited from Queen Elizabeth difficult problems in religion. Almost everyone believed that a kingdom divided in religion was certain to prove unstable and yet unity in religion had not been achieved, despite the Queen's efforts. There was a small Catholic minority, whose power was much exaggerated and feared by the Protestant majority. English Protestants disagreed among themselves. Some believed that Elizabeth's established Church was still insufficiently free of the taint of Catholicism. A few wanted to separate themselves from the ungodly masses as separate congregations of those who had experienced Christ's call. Religious issues were made far more difficult by the fact that the Stuarts ruled over two other kingdoms besides England. In Ireland acceptance of Stuart rule was greatly hindered by the allegiance to Catholicism of the overwhelming majority of the Irish. Scotland had a Presbyterian Church ruled by assemblies instead of bishops. There too religion could easily put the people and Kings who preferred rule by bishops at loggerheads.

Seventeenth century Kings of Britain would have faced difficult problems connected with religion, finance, and their relationships with Parliament whoever they had been. Yet it was not predestined that there would be a Civil War in the 1640s, the execution of a King in 1649 and the deposition of another in 1688. These calamities owed something to the personalities of such Kings as Charles I and James II, but even more to their preferences in religion. In France or Spain religion was a vital bond between the Kings and the majority of their subjects and as such it legitimized and sanctified their rule. Charles I, however, was divided from his subjects by his endorsement of a variant of Protestantism known as Arminianism, which seemed to many people indistinguishable from Catholicism. It did not help either that his French Queen had remained a Catholic. In the next generation, Charles II seemed sympathetic to Catholicism, while his brother James, who succeeded him, was a practising Catholic. It is not an accident that political stability was achieved only after 1688 under monarchs whose Protestant sympathies were beyond question.

I

JAMES I AND CHARLES I

I. Puritans and Catholics

JAMES VI of Scotland, who became James I of England in 1603, had been a King since infancy. The Scotland over which he had reigned had been as turbulent as ever; three out of the four Regents who had ruled during his boyhood had met violent deaths. Against the quarrelsome and bloodthirsty nobles the King had found allies in the ministers of the Kirk. But they were allies who were little to James' taste. He had high notions of his own importance, and of the importance of the office which he held. He firmly believed in the Divine Right of Kings – that Kings are appointed by God[1] and are answerable for their actions, not to their subjects, but to God alone. When, therefore, he was told by Melville, Knox's successor, that he was but 'God's silly vassal', he found it hard to bear with the leaders of the Scottish Kirk.

All this he was now leaving behind – the nobles with their feuds, the elders of the Kirk with their preaching and their lack of respect for bishops and Kings. He was coming, he thought, to a quiet kingdom, to rule over respectful subjects. But appearances are sometimes deceptive. James was perhaps deceived by the language of flattery with which he was everywhere addressed, so different from the way he was treated in Scotland. James believed himself to be a

James I
1603-25

---

[1] In this James was not unusual. Shakespeare makes Richard II say, 'Not all the water in the rough rude sea can wash the balm from an anointed king' (Act III, Scene ii). And note how the doctrine of Divine Right is expressed in the Preface to the Authorized Version of the Bible: 'Great and manifold were the blessings, most dread Sovereign, which Almighty God, the Father of all mercies, bestowed upon us, the people of England, when he first sent Your Majesty's Royal Person to rule and reign over us.'

James I (1566-1625, Reign: King of Scots [as James VI] 1567-1625,
and King of England and Ireland 1603-1625)
(Portrait, c. 1604, attributed to John de Critz)

ruler of wisdom and experience, and he thought – and he let his opinion be known that his new subjects were fortunate to have such a King to rule over them.

James I had certain good qualities. He was a kindly man and full of good intentions. He was a scholar of some note, though he was too fond of 'unbuttoning his royal store of wisdom' for the benefit of his subjects. He also had shortcomings as a King. He was a vain man, called by a contemporary 'the wisest fool in Christendom'. One of his most serious defects was his extravagance, a great contrast with Elizabeth's parsimony. He lavished gifts on his favourites, some of them Scots, and he allowed emotional attraction to distort his judgment of their abilities. He over-promoted them; and they became targets for criticism and brought James' court and government into discredit.

His qualities

Of the surviving servants of the late Queen, the two most distinguished were Sir Robert Cecil and Sir Walter Ralegh. Cecil was at once confirmed in his position as chief minister, and here at least the king made a wise choice. Cecil was made Earl of Salisbury. Ralegh, on the other hand, was soon involved in a plot, formed by his friend Lord Cobham, to dethrone the King in favour of his cousin, Lady Arabella Stuart. The unfortunate lady ended her days in prison, while Sir Walter himself spent thirteen years (1603-16) in the Tower during which time he wrote his *History of the World*.

Robert Cecil

The accession of James brought two blessings to England: the end of the Elizabethan war with Spain, and the union of the kingdoms of England and Scotland. The king himself, in his first speech to Parliament, explained this in characteristic fashion. 'The first of these blessings which God hath jointly with my person sent unto you is outward peace. The second is peace within.... What God hath conjoined, let no man separate. I am the husband, and the whole isle is my lawful wife.' The union of the Crowns of 1603, by putting an end to the prospect of war between England and Scotland, was in itself a great gain. James wished to go farther and sweep away all

Union of the Crowns 1603

trade restrictions between the two countries. But national jealousy, expressed in the English Parliament, thwarted his design.

Peace with Spain 1604

For making peace with Spain James deserves full credit, though it was resented by those persons who had profited from the plunder of Spanish ships on the high seas. It was one of his first actions, and he entrusted the negotiations to Cecil. The Spaniards refused to concede any trade rights with the Spanish Main to England, but Cecil refused to acknowledge their claim to a monopoly. This question was therefore left for the future to decide.

The religious question

The great question of the day, in 1603, was religion. The Anglican Settlement, as made by Elizabeth in the first year of her reign, had endured for her lifetime. But the accession of a new monarch was an obvious moment to reconsider it. James wanted, if possible, to reconcile the Roman Catholics to his regime. The Puritans too had their own suggestions for improving the Church. During his progress from the north James was presented with the so-called Millenary Petition, said to be signed by 1,000 Puritan-inclined clergymen of the Church of England. The petitioners asked, in effect, for some modifications of the Prayer Book; they protested against the use of the sign of the cross in baptism; and they wanted use of the surplice to be optional. Against the opposition of the bishops, the King decided to call a conference of clergy at Hampton Court (1604) to consider these matters, and at the same time to make his own position clear.

Hampton Court Conference 1604

The Puritans hoped much from James, for he had been brought up in the Presbyterian Kirk of Scotland. James was determined to maintain rule of the Church by bishops, since he could control them more easily than he had been able to control the assemblies of the Presbyterian Kirk. He made this clear at the conference. 'If you aim at a Scottish Presbytery,' he told the Puritan clergy, 'it agreeth as well with a monarchy as God with the devil.... Then Jack, Tom, Will and Dick shall meet and at their pleasure censure me and my council ... I thus apply it ... *No bishop, no king.*' Yet most Puritans had no interest in changing the government of the Church, provided that the bishops treated their scruples about matters like wearing the surplice with sensitivity. James commanded that Puritans should be dealt with gently and all but about 90 clergy found it possible to accept his Church settlement, despite his failure to make the changes they had hoped for. It was only this small minority and also a number of separatists who took refuge in Holland. Some of the separatists later sailed in the *Mayflower* to America (1620). For the most part, James' reign was marked by a period of peace in the Church.

There was one very important result of the Hampton Court Conference. It was then that King James appointed a committee to make a new translation of the Bible. The Authorized Version, as it is called, was published in 1611, and did much to shape the development of the English language. It also deeply affected the lives of ordinary men and women, to whom the Bible was their only literature. The old Scripture stories, told in homely yet noble words, sank deep into the hearts of that and succeeding generations.

The Authorized Version 1611

James was anxious to reconcile to his rule not only as many as possible of his Protestant subjects, but also the Roman Catholics. The later Elizabethan laws against them were, as we have seen, extremely harsh. James began by lightening the burden. He at first relaxed the laws against recusants, and allowed priests – so long living in hiding in Catholic manor houses – to go about their work unmolested. These measures soon revealed that the number of Catholics was far greater than had been supposed, and Protestants became alarmed at the large gatherings of Catholics, who no longer feared to go to Mass. The King, in alarm, then changed his policy, and ordered all priests to quit the country (1604). A few Catholics, naturally incensed at this quick change of front, were ready to rebel. It was then that the famous Gunpowder Plot was hatched.

Treatment of Catholics

Robert Catesby, a Midland squire, was the originator of the Gunpowder Plot, and he was joined by several other gentlemen of the west Midlands. Their object was to blow up the Houses of Parliament so that King, Lords, and Commons would perish in

Gunpowder Plot 1605

THE GUNPOWDER PLOT CONSPIRATORS, 1605, BY CRISPIJN VAN DE PASSE THE ELDER
(Guy Fawkes can be seen third from right)

THE GUNPOWDER PLOT
A contemporary print depicting what would have happened if the plot had succeeded.

one terrific conflagration. Then, when the capital was thrown into confusion, the plotters would rise and help to set up a Catholic government.

It was a desperate scheme, and it might have succeeded. That it did not was due to one Tresham, a conspirator less iron-nerved than the rest. He warned his cousin, Lord Monteagle: 'They shall receive a terrible blow, this Parliament, and they shall not see who hurts them.' Such was the warning, and some among the Council suspected the use of gunpowder. One of them examined the cellars under the House of Lords. There he found Guy Fawkes, the sentinel detailed to keep watch over the barrels of gunpowder, which were concealed beneath a load of faggots. It was the evening of the day before the meeting of Parliament. Guy Fawkes had already suspected that 5 Nov. 1605 the plot was betrayed, but he stuck to his post in the faint hope that he might after all succeed in his fearful task. He was seized where he stood, taken to the Tower, and put to the torture. But he would not reveal the names of his accomplices until he knew that they had all been taken or slain. Their rebellion had failed, and Catesby himself was slain. Guy Fawkes was hanged, and to this day his effigy is burnt in our streets on November 5th. Father Garnet, the head of the English Jesuits, was also seized and put to death for complicity in the plot. The horror caused by the discovery of the Gunpowder Plot naturally reacted – like the Smithfield burnings – against the English Catholics, and for two hundred years the evil impression remained. It was long before the average Englishman got rid of the absurd idea that every Catholic was a traitor and every Jesuit a murderer. James himself appreciated that the Plot of 1605 had been the work of a desperate minority and soon reverted to a more tolerant policy towards the Catholic community. His failure to enforce the laws against Catholics in their full rigour was a regular source of complaint in his Parliaments.

2. James I and his Parliaments

First Parliament 1604-10

The first Parliament of James I (1604-10) was the longest in his reign. The House of Commons, James soon found, was a very different body from the compliant assembly he had hoped to find ready to listen to his royal words of wisdom. The members were chosen from the gentry of England – the squire class who ruled the countryside. There were about 500 members, 400 of whom represented the boroughs. The borough members, however, were not usually townsmen, but squires chosen from the neighbourhood.

Divine Right

It is unlikely that James I alienated the Commons by his insistence on his 'Divine Right'. The doctrine of Divine Right was not new. Its clerical and legal exponents found support for it in history and Scripture. Probably no Member of Parliament would have questioned what James said to Parliament in 1610. 'The state of monarchy,' he said, 'is the supremest thing on earth.' The House of Commons, he proceeded, must be careful to confine itself to respectful advice and 'not meddle with the main points of government; that is my craft; to meddle with that were to lesson me. I am now an old king.... I must not be taught my office.' What did worry some MPs, well aware of how parliamentary bodies in France and Spain had declined, was that the Parliament of England too might become redundant. That is why they frequently harked back to the middle ages, when Parliament seemed to have been an important institution. Yet James had no intention of destroying English laws and institutions. He took seriously his Coronation oath to maintain them.

Finance

In the earlier part of James' reign, King and Commons conflicted chiefly about taxation, a matter traditionally under the Commons' control. The king was still expected, as in medieval times, to 'live of his own'; in other words, to meet the expenses of both court and government out of his regular income. This income was derived (i) from feudal dues on landowners and rents on Crown lands; (ii) from the customs, that is, duties paid on goods, e.g. wool and leather, which belonged by ancient custom to the king; and (iii) from Tonnage and Poundage, a separate levy which Parliament granted the king for life at the beginning of every reign, consisting of the duties paid on every tun of wine and pound of merchandise imported into the country. But all this was not nearly enough. James was a spendthrift, and kept up an expensive court. He also had a family to maintain, unlike his predecessor. Further, after the great inflation of the 16th century, the value of money was only half as much as it had been a century earlier. Government was now more active and therefore more costly, and it was no longer realistic to expect the King to manage on the proceeds of traditional sources of revenue. James therefore tried other means of raising money, such as the sale of monopolies. He also imposed, without a parliamentary grant, additional customs duties known as 'impositions'. A merchant called Bate who refused to pay this extra duty imposed on his currants lost his case in the Courts (1606); and James' Book of Rates (1608) contained still more impositions. There was an attempt at an agreement between king and Parliament, known as the Great Contract (1610), by which the king would have received a regular income of £200,000 from parliamentary taxation in return for giving up feudal dues. But the scheme fell through.

Not long after this James dissolved his first Parliament (1610). He called another in 1614, which the humorists called the Addled Parliament, because it did not hatch a single Bill. It sat for only two months, and refused to vote a penny till grievances had been discussed. James dissolved it in anger, and ruled without a Parliament till 1621. The sale of monopolies continued, as did impositions. Titles of honour were put up for sale: baronetcies, for example, cost £1,000 each.

Addled Parliament 1614

James lost his eldest son Prince Henry, and his chief minister Lord Salisbury, in the same year (1612). On the death of Cecil he chose a worthless Scotsman, called Robert Carr, to be the recipient of his confidence. Carr was made Duke of Somerset, and for some years

Death of Cecil 1612

21

he continued to flourish in the sunshine of the royal favour. But after he had been involved in several unpleasant scandals, including a trial for murder, he was disgraced (1616). His successor was George Villiers, a court favourite who was created first Earl and then Duke of Buckingham. He was a worthier, if not a wiser, man than Carr, and the King gave him his confidence.

Buckingham

For the last years of the reign Buckingham had a great influence on the government of England, but James continued to decide the big issues of the day. In 1617 he had Ralegh released from the Tower and sent him on an expedition to Guiana, where, the old adventurer predicted, gold could be found in great quantities. Perhaps James hoped thus to solve his financial problems. The risk was that the expedition might provoke conflict with Spain and Ralegh had to promise not to fight the Spaniards. But the next year he was back in England. He had found no gold, and had killed some Spaniards in a skirmish, and lost his own son. Gondomar, the Spanish ambassador, demanded the head of the old hero. Elizabeth had refused a like request for Drake's death, but James sacrificed Ralegh, and he was executed (1618).

Execution of
Ralegh 1618

The Thirty
Years' War
1618-48

In the year of Ralegh's execution, a storm-cloud burst over Europe. The terrible Thirty Years' War, which devastated Germany, broke out. Frederick of the Palatinate (on the Rhine), who was James' son-in-law, having married his daughter Elizabeth, accepted the offer of the crown of Bohemia (1620) when the Bohemians rebelled against the Habsburg Emperor. Frederick was chosen because he was a Calvinist; but he had little success, and soon lost Bohemia and the Palatinate as well, the latter state being overrun by the Spaniards, who were allies of the Emperor, their King's cousin. James attempted the role of peacemaker. He asked the Spaniards to restore the Palatinate to his son-in-law, and he worked for an Anglo-Spanish alliance to be sealed by the marriage of Prince Charles and the Infanta, daughter of Philip IV of Spain. This alliance, by bridging the Catholic-Protestant divide, might be able to restore peace in

Germany. At the same time, he decided to increase his bargaining power by making a show of force, though he always hoped to avoid war, since he realized that it would be ruinously expensive.

As war could not be waged without money, Parliament had to be summoned (1621). Many grievances had accumulated since their last meeting and James recognized that the Commons should have the opportunity to raise them. They began to attack monopolies, which James, like Elizabeth, had used to reward courtiers. In their search for a weapon against monopolists, the Commons re-asserted their ancient right (not used since 1459) to impeach the king's servants: the Commons made their accusations and the House of Lords acted as judges. This procedure was then used against Francis Bacon, the Lord Chancellor, who was impeached for receiving bribes from those with cases pending in the courts; he was found guilty and deprived of his office. So far the King and the Commons had co-operated amicably, but the Commons had yet to address the King's business. They finally voted a wholly inadequate subsidy, probably feeling that they could not impose a larger burden on their constituents in the middle of an economic depression. Left without clear guidance from the government, they went on to discuss foreign policy, and to petition against the Spanish marriage. Furious when he found out, the King lectured them in his usual strain. He told the members not 'to meddle with anything concerning our government or deep matters of state, and, namely, not to deal with our dearest son's match with the daughter of Spain, nor to touch the honour of that King'. James also reminded the members that their privileges were 'derived from the grace and permission of our ancestors and us'. They replied in a formal Protestation (1621) that their privileges were the 'ancient and undoubted birthright and inheritance of the subjects of England'. Trembling with rage, the King with his own hand tore the offending protest from the Commons' Journal – and dissolved Parliament.

Third Parliament 1621

Prince
Charles in
Spain
A year later, against the King's will, Charles and Buckingham went in disguise to Spain in order to achieve at last the Spanish marriage. They were not allowed to see the Infanta until they had promised concessions for Roman Catholics in England. This they were neither able nor willing to do. So the Prince returned in disgust to England without a Spanish bride, much to the satisfaction of the English people, who organized a display of public rejoicing to celebrate the occasion.

Fourth
Parliament
Buckingham then decided to abandon the Spanish marriage project. He persuaded his master to summon another Parliament (1624), and prepare to join Denmark and Holland, which were already involved in the Thirty Years' War against the Habsburgs. For the moment the minister was popular. He dispatched an army – 'a rabble of raw and poor rascals' – to Holland. But they had few provisions and were left to starve on the island of Walcheren.

Death of
James I
1625
King James did not live to see the end of this ill-fated expedition. He died the same winter (1625).

His character
Posterity has not been merciful to the memory of James I; and the origins of the Civil War have often been traced back to his reign. It has been overlooked that James not only aspired to become the peacemaker of Europe, but also strove to bring peace to Great Britain, that is peace between England and Scotland and also peace among those of different opinions in religion. His efforts were attended by a large measure of success. He did not achieve a fruitful partnership with most of his Parliaments, but nor did he decide to have done with them altogether. The main issue which prevented harmony was finance. Elizabeth had made do with an antiquated system which barely sufficed to support peacetime government and certainly could not stretch to financing any action abroad. Unfortunately, James' extravagant and corrupt court gave his Parliaments every excuse to be mean, but they were in any case inclined to be unrealistic in their estimates of how great an income the King needed. James I bequeathed to his son the intractable problem of how to finance the government of the country.

3. Charles I and Buckingham

Early 17th century Englishmen were well aware that ancient representative institutions were in many countries losing their relevance and importance as rulers threw off checks upon their power and made themselves absolute. In 1625 it was said, 'England is the last monarchy that retains her liberties – let them not perish now!' In England Charles I does not appear to have planned to destroy Parliament and set up an absolute government, but in the later 1620s he found it impossible to work with that institution. He came to the conclusion that it was an obstacle to good government and that if he was to be able to govern at all, he would need to dispense with it. Ultimately, his decision to do without Parliament led to the Civil War. England had experienced civil wars before, most recently the 15th century Wars of the Roses, but the war in Charles I's reign was different. Perhaps the most obvious difference was that it was not simply an English civil war, but rather a war which involved all three of Charles' kingdoms, Scotland and Ireland as well as England.

Charles I 1625-49

His character

Charles I was in many ways an attractive man. His manners were dignified and his private life was beyond reproach. His court was well-ordered and there were none of the scandals that had marked his father's reign. He had strong artistic interests, and was the patron of the architect Inigo Jones and of Van Dyck, who painted the portraits which have made Charles' figure so familiar. But though a man of taste, Charles was an unsatisfactory ruler. Growing up in the shadow of his elder brother Henry, who died of smallpox in 1612, Charles lacked confidence, as his stammer revealed. If his will was crossed, he took refuge in silence, in marked contrast to his father's talkativeness. He was rarely willing to explain his objectives or actions, but took his stand upon his rights and the self-evident purity of his intentions. Such an inaccessible ruler could easily come to be distrusted. Charles was also inflexible. Once committed to them, he clung obstinately to policies and people. He was a King who shunned compromise and invited confrontation.

At his accession, Charles was under the influence of his father's favourite, the Duke of Buckingham. The handsome, dashing, confident Duke had a dozen plans ready to pour into the willing ears of the King. Buckingham was now (1625) committed to a French alliance. The marriage of Charles to Henrietta Maria, sister of Louis XIII, had already been arranged. It was celebrated (by proxy) shortly after Charles' accession and before Parliament could meet to ask awkward questions. Such questions were to be expected, for Buckingham had promised the last Parliament that no relief to English Catholics should follow the French marriage. On the other hand, he had promised Louis XIII (in the marriage treaty) the exact contrary. English Protestants objected to the new Queen because she was a Catholic; they feared she would influence her children in favour of her own faith, and in this respect their fears were fulfilled. The Queen was only fifteen at the time of her marriage, which was at first an unhappy one; but after Buckingham's death she became reconciled to her husband. Henceforth she exerted a strong influence over Charles. Her love of pleasure, and her fondness for dancing and play-acting, gave offence to those of Puritan inclination.

Marriage of Charles I 1625

Charles' first Parliament (1625) met in truculent mood. The Parliament of 1624 had voted a large sum for the war against the Habsburgs, but there was little to show for it and MPs were reluctant to grant the King yet more of their constituents' money. They voted only £140,000 – hardly a tenth of the amount required – to wage a war against Spain. The King felt badly let down, since he was attempting to fight a war which Parliament had wanted. The Commons also voted tonnage and poundage duties, but for one year only, since they wished to resolve the issue of the King's right to impositions, the extra customs duties which the Crown had been collecting since 1606. In the event, the issue was not resolved and the King was never voted tonnage and poundage, but he had no

First Parliament 1625

CHARLES I (1600-1649, REIGN: 1625-1649)
(1631 portrait by Daniel Mytens)

option but to continue to collect these taxes, without which his government could not function. Hence another cause of quarrel between the King and his Parliaments arose.

The King entrusted Buckingham with the conduct of the Spanish

Second Parliament war; Sir Edward Cecil was sent with a fleet to Cadíz. This expedition, owing largely to Buckingham's inefficient organization, was a complete failure, and Cecil returned with nothing to show for the money expended. Charles then decided to call a second Parliament

Sir John Eliot (1626). The leaders of the Commons at this time were Sir John Eliot, Sir Thomas Wentworth and John Pym. Eliot, a fiery Cornishman, made a long speech against Buckingham and his conduct of the war: 'Our honour is ruined, our ships are sunk, our men perished, not by the enemy, not by chance, but by those we trust.' This tirade offended the King, who told the Speaker: 'I would not have the House to question my servants, much less one that is so near me.' The debate went on; Charles tried threats. 'Remember,' he said, 'that Parliaments are altogether in my power for their calling, sitting and dissolution; and therefore as I find the fruits of them good or evil, they are to continue or not to be.' Soon the news arrived that Cardinal Richelieu, the great French minister, had made peace with Spain – a bitter blow to England. After further debate the Commons formally impeached the Duke of Buckingham at the Bar of the House of Lords for misconducting the war. Charles' reply was to dissolve Parliament (1626).

Raising money by a forced loan – which offended the trading community of London – Charles then proceeded to equip more ships and men in order to continue the war. Next year he quarrelled with his brother-in-law, Louis XIII, who not unnaturally asked for the terms of the marriage treaty to be carried out. But instead of granting relief to Catholics, Charles, who was now on bad terms with his

The French War 1627 Queen, actually drove her French attendants from England. By the end of the year (1627) England and France were at war. Buckingham, optimistic as ever, suggested sending a fleet to relieve La Rochelle, the Huguenot stronghold on the Bay of Biscay, which Richelieu was besieging. Buckingham himself commanded the English attack, and landed on the Isle de Re, near La Rochelle. But he could not relieve the town, and retired to England for reinforcements.

Charles now summoned his third Parliament (1628-9). Sir John Eliot thundered against the King's methods of raising money, and defended the rights of the House. Finally the grievances of the Commons were embodied in the Petition of Right (1628), which passed both Houses, and to which the King gave his assent on condition that more money was voted for the French war. This famous Petition, which thus became an Act of Parliament, was intended to limit the King's arbitrary power in four directions; billeting of soldiers, martial law, taxation, and imprisonment. First, he was not to become a military ruler. The members recalled how Rome had fallen 'through the insolency of soldiers'; they knew the country was full of complaints of the behaviour of Buckingham's troops who had been billeted on private citizens. Henceforth such billeting was to be illegal: 'no man is forced to take soldiers, but inns, and they be paid for them.' At the same time, courts martial were forbidden to try civilians. These two clauses of the Petition of Right have been called the 'charter of the most civilian nation of Europe'; and a suspicion of armies was to be characteristic of England for the next two centuries. Another clause of the Petition provided that 'no man hereafter be compelled to make or yield any gift, loan, benevolence, tax or such-like charge, without common consent by Act of Parliament'. Now the king had not only raised such taxes, but had recently imprisoned eighty gentlemen for refusing to pay them; he had done so 'without any cause showed', and he had not brought them to trial. The Petition made such arbitrary imprisonment illegal.

In the same year Buckingham went down to Portsmouth to embark once more for France. While he was there, he was assassinated by a discontented officer named Felton. London broke into unseemly rejoicings at the news; and the mob cheered when the duke's coffin passed through the streets. Charles was distracted with grief; but he went on with the war. The fleet sailed for La Rochelle,

Third Parliament 1628-9

Petition of Right 1628

Murder of Buckingham 1623

End of
the third
Parliament
1629

only to find that Richelieu had constructed a mole across the harbour to prevent the relief of the city. The expedition was thus foiled, and the Huguenots surrendered to the Cardinal (1628). Next year the King's third Parliament came to an end in dramatic fashion. The Commons were discussing grievances when the King decided on an adjournment. As Sir John Eliot rose to address the House, the Speaker (who wished to carry out the King's orders) attempted to leave and so end the debate. Thereupon two members forcibly held him down in his chair while the Commons hurriedly passed Eliot's Three Resolutions (2 March 1629), which condemned 'innovations in religion' and the 'introduction of Popery', and declared that anyone proposing or paying tonnage and poundage not granted by Parliament was a traitor to 'the kingdom and commonwealth'. When the resolutions had been passed, the Speaker was released, the doors were opened, and Parliament was dissolved (1629). After this scene in the House Charles proclaimed that the Commons had been attempting 'to exert a universal, overswaying power, which belongs only to me and not to them'. This was not what the protesters in the Commons saw themselves as doing. They believed that they were defending the Protestant religion and the constitutional arrangements that had prevailed in Queen Elizabeth's day. But it seemed to Charles that Parliament's attitude towards supplies and its attacks on his religious policy made it impossible to carry on the government at all. He was 'ashamed that his cousins of France and Spain should have accomplished a work (an absolute monarchy) which he had scarcely begun'. Many Puritans migrated overseas to New England rather than live under the non-parliamentary government which now followed.

4. 'Personal' Government

Having failed to rule with the help of Parliament, Charles now decided to rule without a Parliament, nor did he summon another for eleven years. His first business was to bring the war with France and Spain to an end, for obviously he could not hope to finance it. Peace was accordingly made with both countries in 1630. Compared with the rule of a King like Henry VIII, Charles' rule was mild. Charles did not, like Henry VIII, send men to the scaffold; there were no hangings and burnings. In some respects the severity of the laws was relaxed. Torture, which had been employed against the misguided but heroic Guy Fawkes, was discontinued under Charles I and has not since been used in England. The country was, in some respects, becoming more humane; and Charles himself was not a cruel man. His personal rule is sometimes called 'The Eleven Years' Tyranny'. Yet it was no tyranny if judged either by contemporary European or by Tudor standards. Charles was also anxious that his regime should be seen as one that abided by the laws of the realm. But it offended an influential section of his subjects. Because it failed, he had to pay the penalty.

One of the King's chief advisers during these eleven years was William Laud, bishop of London, a former President of St. John's College, Oxford. Laud was made Archbishop of Canterbury (1633) and henceforth his influence was important in both Church and State. He directed the religious policy of the government, and after the death in 1635 of the Treasurer, Weston, Juxon, another bishop, became responsible for the finances of the kingdom. Laud's great friend was Sir Thomas Wentworth, a parliamentary leader who had formerly opposed the King through distrust of Buckingham. Wentworth became disgusted with the unconstructive approach of some of the leaders of the Commons in 1628-9: to him, as to Laud, 'order (in Church and State) was Heaven's first law'. And Wentworth was also well suited to be a servant of the King, since he was a man of autocratic temper. The murder of Buckingham, moreover, removed his chief objection to the King's government, and seeing his opportunity he became one of Charles' foremost servants. Charles made him a peer (1628) and President of the Council of the North

Character of Charles' rule

William Laud

Wentworth

(1628-32), and then Lord Deputy of Ireland (1632-9). In Ireland he ruled with a rod of iron, for he raised an army to enforce his will. 'I am for *thorough* my lord,' he wrote to Laud, whom he urged to follow the same relentless methods. But it was easier to subject a divided country like Ireland with an army than to rule England without one.

'Thorough'

The two chief questions at issue were finance and religion. Let us consider these in turn. The king broke the spirit, but characteristically not the letter, of the provisions of the Petition of Right, to which he had so recently given his assent. He imprisoned Sir John Eliot – 'the champion of Parliamentary privilege' – and other M.P.s for seditious words in the recent Parliament; and Eliot, who refused to apologize, died in the Tower. The King's chief difficulties being financial, he raised money by hated methods such as the sale of monopolies to companies (not to individuals, since that had been declared illegal under James I). His lawyers, too, dug up old laws which had never been repealed, and so Charles 'wrested the law to his authority'. The ancient Forest Laws were revived: it was found that many landowners had built on or enclosed land formerly part of royal forests, and they were fined by the Star Chamber. Many gentlemen of means were also forced to receive – in accordance with Edward I's practice – the 'honour' of knighthood – and had to pay for the privilege. Such expedients were more irksome to his subjects than lucrative to the King. Far and away the most important branch of the revenue was the taxes on trade, which the King continued to collect despite the fact that he had not been voted them by Parliament. The King was able to take advantage of a growth of trade in the period of peace which his treaties with France and Spain ushered in.

Passing money

The tax which aroused most wrath was the levying of Ship Money. Charles wished to repair the ships of the Royal Navy, which had been so neglected in his father's time that the fine Navy which had beaten the Armada had almost disappeared; he hoped to bring the Navy up to the level of the Dutch and French fleets and to protect the shores against pirates. The first writ of Ship Money (1634) was issued to the

Ship money

ports only, in accordance with custom. But from 1635 onwards writs were issued to the inland counties as well, and it was this innovation which aroused opposition. It was argued that Ship Money had been levied without consent of Parliament, and was therefore contrary to the Petition of Right. John Hampden, a Buckinghamshire squire and the friend of Pym and Oliver Cromwell, refused to pay the tax. Hampden's case came (1638) before the Exchequer Court, and a bare majority of the judges decided against him. They argued that it was the King's legal right to impose Ship Money in a case of emergency, and that 'His Majesty is the sole judge, both of the danger, and when and how the same is to be prevented and avoided'.

John Hampden's case 1638

It was, however, by their religious policy that Charles and Laud did most to create bitter enemies of their rule. Charles' version of Protestantism was very different from that of his father or Queen Elizabeth. From the start of his reign he had promoted as bishops only those clergy who believed that not preaching, but the sacraments were the heart of true worship. They began to speak of the altar, not the communion table, and they insisted that proper reverence should be paid to it and that it should therefore be railed off. Worship was to appeal to the senses: hence Archbishop Laud's love for beautiful things, for stained glass and ornament, and for fine music. He had a reverence for sacred places, which many Englishmen had not. He aimed to restore order and decency in the Church and its services; he stopped, for example, the custom of using St. Paul's Cathedral as a meeting-place for gossips and merchants.

Religious policy of Laud

The plain services and bare buildings which had been favoured since 1559 were alike abhorrent to Laud. Like most of his enemies, Laud believed that it was important to achieve uniformity of ceremonial in all English churches and he strove to force his critics to conform to his views. Though a man of taste and learning, he had a narrow, pedantic mind, and little human sympathy. In addition he had a hasty temper and a sharp tongue, and he could not (says

Clarendon, who later wrote a history of these years) 'debate anything without some commotion'. In short, Laud was a man well suited to polarise those of different opinions in the Church of England. To his enemies his version of religion seemed more or less indistinguishable from Roman Catholicism. Though Laud protested strongly against the influence of the Catholics surrounding the Queen, his enemies believed him to be undoing the godly work of the Reformation and reverting to a religion that was not truly Christian at all.

Laud kept a close watch on the press, and fined many speakers and authors critical of his religious policies by means of the Court of High Commission (which had been set up by Elizabeth). One of his victims was William Prynne, a barrister, who had written a long book about the wickedness of stage-plays, and who was eventually condemned, along with three others, for libelling the bishops (1637). These men were sentenced to pay a heavy fine, to be imprisoned for life, and to have their ears cropped. But the people of London showed their disapproval by giving the victims a great ovation in the pillory. Londoners had no quarrel with the principle that men should be punished for holding the wrong religious opinions, but they agreed with Prynne rather than with Laud about what the wrong religious opinions were.

Strict discipline was the key-note of Laud's system. The Court of High Commission, of which he was president, punished a great variety of offenders, from the clergyman who had dared to preach without a surplice to the courtier who had ill-treated his wife, or the innkeeper who had allowed drinking on Sundays. Laud's strict rule, of course, was detested by the pleasure-loving. But it was hated still more by traditional English Protestants, labelled Puritans by Laud and his allies, who compared it with the work of the Inquisition. During these years (1629-40) thousands of Puritans emigrated to America rather than live under what they considered a tyranny. So they went to Massachusetts – and there set up an equally intolerant religious regime of their own!

Puritan emigration

The year 1637 – with Prynne's case (religion) and Hampden's case (finance) – was the real beginning of the crisis of Charles I's reign. Milton in his *Lycidas* (1637) expressed the Puritan's view of the Laudian system: 'the hungry sheep look up and are not fed', while 'the grim wolf (Rome) with privy paw, daily devours apace, and nothing said'. There are many indications that Charles' rule was far from popular in England, particularly the applause with which Prynne and his fellow martyrs were greeted in the towns through which they passed on their way to their separate distant prisons. In the absence of Parliament, however, it is hard to see how concerted opposition could have been organised. Charles I benefited from the Tudors' success in making serious rebellion very hard to bring about. It was therefore not the English, but the Scots who brought about the collapse of Charles I's personal government.

Charles and Laud decided that the northern kingdom must be brought into line with England. Without consulting the Scots, Laud therefore prepared a liturgy, similar to the English Prayer Book, which was to be used instead of Knox's Liturgy in all Scottish churches. This provoked a riot in St. Giles', Edinburgh. When the Dean 'in the whites' (surplice) was about to read the new liturgy for the first time, Jenny Geddes flung a stool at his head. Laud also decided that bishops, originally imposed on the Kirk by James I, instead of the Presbyteries should rule over the Scottish Kirk. These measures provoked a national resistance in Scotland, and the National Covenant[2] (1638) was now signed enthusiastically throughout the land. The wording of the Covenant throws a lurid light on the fierce passions of the Scots, particularly in the passage where the Anglican system is compared with that of Rome. It condemned Laud and all his works, together with 'the usurped authority of that Roman anti-

Laud and Scotland

The National Covenant 1638

---

[2] The Covenant had originally been drawn up in 1581, during the period of papal aggression.

Christ ... all his tyrannous laws made against our Christian liberty his devilish mass ... his holy water, baptizing of bells, conjuring of spirits, crossing, anointing ... his worldly monarchy and wicked hierarchy, his erroneous and bloody decrees made at Trent, with all the subscribers and approvers of that cruel and bloody band conjured against the Kirk of God.'

The Covenanters meant what they said, and their deeds were as earnest as their words. They raised an army and dared the King to invade Scotland. Charles replied by marching north with an ill-equipped host to wage what is called the First Bishops' War (1639). But he never entered Scotland, for he soon saw that his men were no match for such an enemy. By the Treaty of Berwick he agreed to let the Scots settle their own affairs. The Covenanters, however, did not disband their army.

First Bishops' War 1639

This failure, together with growing opposition from the English, who showed uncharacteristic sympathy for the Scots, convinced Charles that the situation was growing desperate. He decided to recall Wentworth from Ireland, and from the moment of his return Wentworth took the first place in the King's counsels, thanks to the determination that he showed. To him the issue seemed straightforward: the Scots were rebels and as such must be crushed.

Wentworth recalled

The fateful year 1640 opened. Wentworth was made Earl of Strafford. His haughty manners aroused fierce hatred in England; his known ruthlessness made him as much feared as he was hated. In view of the King's lack of money, he advised him to summon a Parliament. The Short Parliament (April–May 1640) met and was asked to vote money. The members, as usual, demanded redress of grievances before granting supplies, and Charles impatiently dismissed them. He then tried, with Strafford's aid, to carry on as before. But that summer the Scots, suspecting Strafford's intention to treat them as he had treated the Irish, were again in arms. They invaded England before the King could strike, and so came the Second Bishops' War (June-October 1640). Again forced by

Short Parliament 1640 (Apr-May)

Second Bishops' War 1640 (June-Oct)

THOMAS WENTWORTH, 1ST EARL OF STRAFFORD (1593-1641)
(Portrait by Sir Anthony Van Dyck)

superior numbers to give way, Charles signed the Treaty of Ripon, by which the Scottish army was left on English soil – at his expense, £850 per day.

Strafford again advised the summoning of Parliament, and indeed there was nothing else to be done. Charles had no money and no army

Meeting of
the Long
Parliament
Nov. 1640
worth the name. He must, if possible, come to terms with his English subjects. So the famous Long Parliament of the Puritan Revolution assembled at Westminster in November 1640. Scarcely had it done so when Strafford, by order of the Lords, was arrested and thrown into prison.

5. The Long Parliament of the Puritan Revolution

The meeting of the Long Parliament (as it was afterwards called) in November 1640 was ominous for Charles I. The leaders of the Commons were determined on reform; they meant to put an end to what they saw as the King's unconstitutional methods in both Church and State. Charles himself, though he seldom faced facts, saw that some concessions would be necessary. But a real settlement was not achieved, chiefly because tempers were rising and the King and the leaders of the Commons did not trust each other. Charles knew that Pym, the acknowledged leader of the Commons, and his friends were in league with the Scots, whose army stationed in the north forced him to negotiate with Parliament from a position of weakness. He believed it his duty to pass on the royal power intact to his son. Pym he therefore saw as a traitor and subverter of the royal rights. To
Pym Pym it seemed that Charles' concessions were insincere and would be withdrawn should Charles ever gain the upper hand. To ensure that the King did not regain the initiative, Pym found himself compelled to limit the King's powers in a revolutionary fashion, which appeared to justify all the King's suspicions of him.

John Pym was a squire of Somerset. His enemies nicknamed him 'King Pym'. He was 'the first great popular organizer', for he used the press, the petition, and even the platform to support his cause and had close relations with the popular leaders of the city of London. He now led the attack on the chief instruments of the late personal government. The judges who had upheld Charles' financial exactions in the Courts were arrested and imprisoned, and so was Archbishop Laud, who was beheaded in 1645. But the principal victim was Strafford. He was charged with having tried to 'subvert the fundamental laws and government of England and Ireland, and instead thereof to introduce an arbitrary and tyrannical government against law'. In March 1641 he was brought to Westminster Hall to be tried for high treason. But his accusers were at once faced with a difficult point. Strafford may have tried to 'subvert the laws'; but treason meant treason to the King, and had Strafford been a traitor to Charles? It was difficult to prove that he had, and as the trial proceeded it became clear that the verdict would be Not Guilty. But the majority in the House was determined that Strafford should die. Parliament therefore passed a special Bill of Attainder, condemning the minister to death without trial.

Trial of Strafford 1641

The Lords passed the Bill of Attainder, and it remained for the King to give or to withhold his consent. Some may think that it was Charles' duty to risk his life to defend Strafford. But the London mob raged round Whitehall, howling for blood. Charles feared for the safety of the Queen and his children, and he gave way. 'If my own person only were in danger,' he told the Council, with tears in his eyes, 'I would gladly venture it to save Lord Strafford's life.' Three days later the earl was led to his execution (May 1641) in the presence of a dense crowd of people who had come to witness the end of 'Black Tom Tyrant'. No man ever died more bravely. 'I thank my God', he said, as he prepared to die, 'I am not afraid of death, but do as cheerfully put off my doublet at this time as ever I did when I went to bed.' The executioner offered to cover his eyes with a handkerchief. 'Thou shalt not bind my eyes,' said Strafford, 'for I will see it done.' And so he placed his head upon the block. His misfortune, wrote Laud, was that 'he served a mild and gracious prince, who knew not how to be, or be made great'.

Execution of Strafford 1641

That summer Parliament was busy passing a number of Acts intended to make non-parliamentary government impossible for the future. One Act declared that the present Parliament could not be dissolved without its own consent; another – the Triennial Act – that in future Parliaments should be called every three years. The three Courts by which the King's government had carried out its religious and financial measures were abolished – the Star Chamber, the Court of High Commission, and the Council of the North. Finally Ship Money and other arbitrary forms of taxation were declared illegal. These abolitions of the year 1641 were the permanent, constructive work of the Long Parliament; nor were the institutions then destroyed restored with the monarchy in 1660.

The Royal Tyranny destroyed

Meanwhile, another Bill had come up for discussion. A petition was presented to Parliament praying for the ending of episcopacy (i.e. the rule of the Church by bishops) 'in all its roots and branches'. The thorough-going Protestant members considered the petition, and a 'Root-and-Branch' Bill (1641) was prepared, but it fell through. For now a new factor came into play. Hitherto a large majority, both of Lords and Commons, had been united in their opposition to the King. But this Bill divided Parliamentarians for the first time. There were many who began to fear that the Commons leaders were demanding too many changes; and a moderate party now sprang up. It was out of this debate on the Root-and-Branch Bill that the germs of the future Parliamentarian and Royalist parties were formed. The men who wanted further change in Church and state – the Parliamentarians – included Pym, Hampden, and Oliver Cromwell. The chief figures on the Royalist side resisting further change were Lord Falkland and Sir Edward Hyde, afterwards the famous Earl of Clarendon, the future Chancellor and historian.

The 'Root-and-Branch' Bill 1641

Parliament adjourned for six months, but met again at the end of October. It was at this point that the third of Charles' kingdoms, Ireland, made its fatal contribution to the unfolding of events. Now that the stern hand of Strafford was withdrawn, the crushed Irish had risen against their lords. There was a sudden rebellion; it was rumoured that thousands of Protestants had been massacred in cold

Irish Rebellion 1641

blood. When this news was received in London, it served to increase the already prevalent hysterical fears of popery. But the Irish rebellion also raised a political and constitutional issue of the utmost importance. No Englishman doubted that the revolt would have to be put down by military force. But who should command the army that would put it down? All precedents suggested that the King should exercise command, but some in the Commons no longer trusted Charles and feared that he would use any army to crush his opponents in Parliament.

Therefore the Commons leaders drew up a Grand Remonstrance in November 1641, in which they recited the past acts of the King and his servants to which they objected – there were 201 items – and stated a programme for the future. Their aim was to convince opinion that the King could not be trusted and that he could not be permitted control of the armed forces in future. Some of the clauses prayed the king to reduce the power of the bishops and to remove 'oppressions in religion'. Another clause asked His Majesty to employ ministers 'such as the Parliament may have cause to confide in', a clause which threatened the King's right to choose his ministers. All this shows that the Commons leaders had considerably advanced their demands. During the months from November 1640 to September 1641 they had succeeded in placing constitutional checks on the King's power. From November 1641 to August 1642 they seemed to Charles bent on seizing control of both Church and State, until they forced Charles to reply: 'If I granted your demands, I should be no more than the mere phantom of a king.' The Grand Remonstrance was so revolutionary that it passed by a majority of only eleven. More and more MPs were worried about the destruction of England's ancient constitution which Pym and his associates appeared to be carrying out. In fact, Pym and his associates were also attached to the ancient constitution, but they felt that they had to safeguard it against a King whom they did not trust.

Grand Remembrance Nov. 1641

The situation, by the end of 1641, was dangerous in the extreme. On the one hand, the Queen and the swaggering former soldiers of the Court were urging Charles to strike at King Pym and his fellow leaders before it was too late. On the other hand, London was a stronghold of anti-popish feeling, and it was the London merchants who had felt the weight of Charles' taxation most heavily. The London 'prentices' and the King's swordsmen were itching to get at one another's throats. Nevertheless, Pym proceeded steadily on his

Militia Bill way. A Militia Bill was therefore brought in, and – contrary to all English law and custom – it took the command of the military forces out of the King's hands. To this Charles of course refused his consent.

The Five
Members
Jan. 1642
Early in January 1642 he took the Queen's advice, and instructed the Attorney-General to impeach Pym, Hampden, and three other leading members of the Commons. The members were alarmed, but Charles promised them 'on the word of a King' that no violence should be done them. The next day (4 January 1642) he went down to the House with 400 swordsmen. He left his guard at the door, and walked in accompanied only by Prince Rupert, his German nephew. But the five members, warned of his intention, had fled by river. There was a dead silence as the King looked round. He asked the Speaker, Lenthall, where the missing members were. 'I have neither eyes to see,' Lenthall replied, 'nor tongue to speak in this place, but as this House shall direct me.' There was another pause as Charles scanned the benches. 'I see', he said at last, 'all the birds are flown. I do expect you will send them to me as soon as they shall return hither.' Then, amid cries of 'Privilege, privilege', he walked out.

Charles
leaves
London
1642
By this act, the King appeared to have given in to those who were urging him to use force against the leaders of the Commons. Any hope of reconciliation was now very faint. The proposals of the King and the Parliamentary leaders were not from now on about finding a formula for a settlement, but were designed to win over support in the country for the appeal to arms that was imminent. The King left his

capital on 10 January, sent the Queen out of the country, and took up his quarters at York.

If the King succeeded in gathering supporters, it was above all because of his promise to defend the established Church, which seemed in increasing danger from Pym and his Parliamentarians. Since the Scots had been paid off in the summer of 1641, Pym's only defence against the swashbucklers round the Queen had been the Londoners. Many of them were determined to get rid of the bishops, to suppress the Prayer Book and finally to create a fully reformed Church. The enemies of this Puritan vision saw it as associated particularly with closely cropped artisans and apprentices in the city of London. This is how the members of the Parliamentarian party acquired the label 'Roundheads'. The name also indicated a fear that Parliament's attack on the rights of the King and hierarchy in the Church would lead on to the undermining of the social order and rule by the *roundheaded* classes. The Parliamentarian leaders, who wore their hair long, were aware of the danger, but saw no other defence against a King who seemed surrounded by Catholics and crypto-Catholics, many of whom were former soldiers anxious to appeal to violence. Hence the King's supporters acquired the label 'Cavaliers'.

In the early months of 1642 Parliament claimed the control of the militia and secured the command of the fleet. During the spring and summer of 1642 both sides were busy raising troops. The great strength of the Parliamentary cause was London. The city contained a tenth of the population of England – 500,000 out of five million. The number of troops which London provided was more than sufficient to quell any Royalist opposition in the surrounding country. The London 'train-bands' (the trained companies of citizen soldiers) therefore protected the Parliamentary leaders during the eight months that the King was gathering his army in the north (January-August 1642).

DATE SUMMARY: STUART PERIOD I
(1603-42)

BRITAIN AND IRELAND   EUROPE, ASIA, AND AMERICA

JAMES I (1603-25)

1604 Hampton Court Conference
1605 Gunpowder Plot

                1607 VIRGINIA
                1608 Quebec (French)
                1609 Hudson River (Dutch)
                1610 Newfoundland
                      Hudson's Bay

                1610 Louis XIII, King of France

1611 Ulster Settlement
     Authorized Version of Bible
1612 Robert Cecil, Lord Salisbury *died*.
1614 Addled Parliament
1618 Ralegh executed

                1618 Thirty Years' War begins
                1619 Virginia Assembly
                1620 PILGRIM FATHERS

1621 Bacon impeached   1621 Philip IV, King of Spain
1623 Prince Charles in Spain   1623 Amboyna Massacre

                1624 Richelieu, chief minister,
                      France

CHARLES I (1625-49)

1625-9 First Three Parliaments   1627 Barbados
1628 Petition of Right   1628 Massachusetts Bay Company
1629-40 'Personal' Government
1632-9 Wentworth in Ireland
1633 Laud Archbishop

                1633 British on R. Hooghly
                1634 Maryland

1638 Hampden (Ship Money) Trial verdict
1639 First Bishops' War   1639 Madras
1640 Short Parliament ; 2nd Bishops' War
     LONG PARLIAMENT meets
1641 Strafford executed
     Grand Remonstrance
     Irish Rebellion
1642 Attempted arrest of 5MPs
     Start of Civil War

II

THE CIVIL WAR AND THE REBUBLIC

1. The Defeat of the King

IT was in a stern and sad mood that the leaders of England drew their swords against each other in the late summer of 1642. A few there were, like the dashing courtiers round the King, who were eager for the fight. But for the most part men went into the great struggle in the spirit of the Puritan gentleman who wrote to his friend – a Royalist – in these words: 'The great God, who is the searcher of my heart, knows with what reluctance I go upon this service, and with what perfect hatred I look upon war without an enemy. We are both on the stage, and we must act the parts assigned to us in this tragedy; let us do it in a way of honour, without personal animosities.' The Civil War

A spirit of loyalty to the king caused many to side with him when it came to actual war. 'I have eaten the King's bread and served him over thirty years,' said Sir Edmund Verney, 'and I will not do so base a thing as to forsake him.' A third of the House of Commons, and three-quarters of the Lords sided with Charles. But many, on both sides, were half-hearted, and feared the issue of the war, whatever it might be. Lord Saville expressed this feeling when he said: 'I would not have the king trample on the Parliament, nor the Parliament lessen him so much as to make a way for the people to rule us all.' Such men hoped against hope that war might be avoided by negotiation. In many counties there was a strong neutralist movement as the gentry did their best to insulate their local communities from the effects of war. But neutrals tended to become victims of attack by partisans on both sides and in the end all attempts to maintain neutrality collapsed. Spirit of the combatants

Maps like the one on page 46 show Parliament in control of the wealthy areas north and south of London, East Anglia, the

Parliament
King

0   100km
0   50miles

SCOTLAND

Newcastle

Hull
Leeds

Chester   Nottingham

EAST

Northampton
×Edge Hill   ANGLIA

WALES   Oxford (K.)
              ×Chalgrove
                          LONDON

Devizes   ×Newbury

Portsmouth

CORNWALL   Plymouth

1642-3

The opposing forces
Midlands, and the West Riding of Yorkshire, of the then small manufacturing towns, like Birmingham, Manchester, and Colchester, of the seaports (e.g. Hull and Portsmouth) and, above all, of London itself. In some ways, though, the map is misleading. Parliament was indeed able to raise money and troops from these areas, but that is not to say that the inhabitants were its enthusiastic supporters. Kent, for example, was Parliamentarian because, given the proximity of London and the distance of the King's armies, it could not realistically be anything else. The Kentish gentry seem to have included many of Royalist sympathies and even more neutrals. The King had on his side the less wealthy regions of the north, the west,

46

Parliament
King

0   100km
0   50miles

Philiphaugh ✗
SCOTLAND
Newcastle
Carlisle (K.)
Scarborough (K.)
Marston Moor ✗ York
Preston
Bolton Pontefract (K.)
Newark (K.)
Lichfield (K.)
✗ Naseby
WALES
Gloucester
Oxford
Pembroke
LONDON
Taunton ✗ Langport
Exeter Lyme
Lostwithiel
Plymouth
After the Campaign of 1644

ENGLAND AND
WALES: CIVIL WAR

and Cornwall. This was not necessarily an insuperable disadvantage, since successful military advances from these areas were likely to embolden the many potential Royalists which all areas contained, as happened when Charles' forces advanced from the south-west in 1643. Though the names *Roundhead* and *Cavalier* suggest that the two sides were composed of different social groups, this does not appear to have been the case. Parliamentarians thought of their enemies as military-minded, mounted aristocrats, as if Prince Rupert were the typical Royalist, but townsmen could be Royalist too: Bristol was not unhappy under Royalist rule after its capture in 1643 and even London had become a stronghold for Pym only after a purge of the City government in late 1641 and in 1642. Royalists thought of Parliamentarians as paving the way for rule by the lower social orders, but it is misleading to make too much of the Parliamentarian sympathies of ports such as Hull and Plymouth, which could not easily opt for the King in view of Parliament's control of the navy. That the navy was on Parliament's side shows how much it owed to aristocrats, since the navy followed the lead of its commander, the Earl of Warwick. In its dependence on the likes of Essex and Manchester among the peers and Hampden and Cromwell from among the gentry for its generals Parliament was not dissimilar from its opponents.

Next to the support of London, Parliament's most important asset was the navy, which made it almost impossible for the King to get help from abroad, though the Queen did succeed in pawning the Crown jewels in the Netherlands and landing shiploads of arms under Dutch protection. Thanks to the navy, Parliament derived a large income from taxes on trade. Charles depended heavily on private generosity. The colleges at Oxford and a few at Cambridge melted down their valuable plate for him, and many an old county family made large donations, including some of the greatest, such as the Marquises of Newcastle and Worcester.

The numbers engaged in the war amounted at times to more than one in ten of all adult males. In the campaigning season 120,000 to 140,000 men might be under arms. The men were recruited by local gentry who were empowered, by King or Parliament, to raise

Officers and men

regiments of foot or troops of horse. The foot soldiers were divided into pikemen and musketeers.[3] The pikemen carried a sword and a sixteen-foot pike. The musketeers also carried a sword, besides the clumsy weapon from which, with a great deal of trouble, they

---

[3] The bayonet had not yet been invented, so the pikemen and musketeers had not yet been amalgamated into one.

managed to fire a few bullets. It took a long time to load and fire a musket, the powder having to be poured down the muzzle first. The rank and file had no experience of war, but many of the officers on both sides had served in the armies of Holland or Sweden in the Thirty Years' War.

Charles made his nephew, Prince Rupert (son of the Elector Palatine), general of the Royalist Horse. Rupert was a dashing young man, but very inexperienced for such a command; he was only twenty-three. 'He should have someone to advise him,' wrote the Queen, 'for, believe me, he is yet very young and self-willed.' The general of the Parliamentary army was the Earl of Essex, son of Elizabeth's favourite, and the only man capable of holding Parliament's forces together. The King himself commanded the Royalist army, but he was as poor a general as he was a ruler. His weak and irresolute character did not inspire confidence, and this was obvious even to the Queen, who wrote to him: 'Take a good resolution and pursue it. To begin and then to stop is your ruin – experience shows it you.' *Prince Rupert*

Essex

Charles raised the royal standard at Nottingham on 22 August 1642, the anniversary of Bosworth Field; but the standard was blown down the same night – an evil omen for the King. Essex, with 20,000 men, was at Northampton, guarding the road to London. Charles moved his army westwards, with the object of recruiting more men before marching on London. Essex marched parallel to the King and reached the Severn at Worcester. But when, at Shrewsbury, the King turned and began his march on London, Essex also turned south-east and intercepted the King at Edgehill, fifteen miles south of Warwick. Beneath the wooded slopes of the hill, the first battle of the Civil War was fought (August 1642). Prince Rupert routed the Parliamentary horse, but, as on later occasions, he pursued too far, and so lost his advantage. The battle was therefore indecisive, and Charles was able to continue his march on the capital. He actually reached the outskirts at Turnham Green, but the London train-bands at this critical *Battle of Edgehill 1642* moment turned out in force to oppose him. He therefore retired to Oxford, which he made his headquarters for the next three years. He thus lost the best chance he ever had of concluding the war at a blow, and he never got so near London again with his army.

In 1643 the Royalists planned a threefold attack on London from The the north, the west, and from Oxford; but the King's armies usually campaign had local priorities and were reluctant to march on towards London of 1643 while towns held out for Parliament behind them. The Marquis of Newcastle overran most of the north for the King, and shut up old Lord Fairfax and his son Sir Thomas in Hull. He then advanced into Lincolnshire, where he received a check. The Parliamentary armies of East Anglia had been organized into the 'Eastern Association', which was kept together by the genius of a Huntingdon Oliver squire. This was Oliver Cromwell, who was the only great military Cromwell leader produced by this war, with the exception of Prince Rupert. Born and bred in the country, Cromwell had a countryman's knowledge of men and horses; and these gifts, combined with his own peculiar energy and earnestness, helped to make him the chosen leader of the East Anglian Parliamentarians. His famous troopers were all sternly disciplined; no gambling and swearing, no drunkenness and no plundering were allowed among this unusual army. Newcastle found he could not advance far against Cromwell's troops, so he turned back into Yorkshire to besiege Hull. But the Roundheads followed him, and Hull was relieved.

A similar campaign took place at the same time in the west of England. Sir Ralph Hopton, the Royalist general, led the men Hull and of Cornwall and Devon towards London, but the farthest point Plymouth eastward which they reached was Roundway Down, outside Devizes. The western troops decided to return home, for Plymouth, supplied by sea, still held out behind them.

In central England there were several Cavalier raids from Oxford, and in a skirmish at Chalgrove Field, near Thame, John Hampden, the Parliamentarian leader, was mortally wounded. The advance of

OLIVER CROMWELL (1599-1658)
(Portrait by Robert Walker)

the King's main army was, however, held up by the resistance of Gloucester, and Charles therefore began the siege of this town. Essex marched from London to its relief, and having succeeded in his task, raced back to the capital across the Berkshire Downs. Charles, also coming from Gloucester by another route, blocked his way at Newbury. But Essex cut his way through and reached London. At

Siege of
Gloucester

51

Newbury fell the noble Lord Falkland, who so hated to shed the blood of his countrymen that he rode into the battle with sword sheathed. A Parliamentarian bullet ended the career of 'that incomparable young man', as he was called by his friend, the statesman and historian, Lord Clarendon. 'Whosoever leads such a life needs not care upon how short warning it be taken from him.'[4]

Battle of Newbury 1643

The end of the year 1643 seemed to promise well for the Royalists. True, they had not taken London, neither had Hull, Gloucester, nor Plymouth fallen. But apart from this they now held most of England except East Anglia and the Home Counties round London. The morale of Parliament's supporters was at a low ebb: a number of MPs had gone over to the King. It was then that Pym played his last card for the Parliamentary cause. He made a treaty with the Scottish Covenanters, by which the Scots promised to send an army of 20,000 men to fight against the King. In return for this help, which the English would pay for, Parliament had to accept the Solemn League and Covenant, by which it was agreed that a Presbyterian Church should be set up in England. Three months later Pym died.

Solemn League and Covenant Sept. 1643

In January 1644 the Scottish army invaded England and laid siege to York, where a Roundhead army, under the Earl of Manchester, soon joined them. In the summer Prince Rupert rode north to the rescue, taking a route through Lancashire. His Cavaliers massacred the defenders of Bolton and sacked the town, this being one of the most brutal episodes of the Civil War. He then relieved York. Eight miles from the City he came upon the Scottish and Roundhead armies on Marston Moor (July 1644). There followed the biggest battle of the war, in which perhaps 45,000 troops were involved. It was already evening when the Parliamentary army charged down on the Royalists. Cromwell's well-trained East Anglians were worthy of

Battle of Marston Moor 1644

---

[4] Clarendon, *History of the Great Rebellion*

their leader; his men of religion were now a match for the 'men of honour' whom Rupert led, though Cromwell, wounded in the neck, required reinforcement by a body of Scots at a crucial moment. The Prince's famous horsemen were put to flight; 'the Lord made them as stubble to our swords', wrote Cromwell. When he had scattered the Royalist horse, Cromwell turned and came to the relief of the Scottish pikemen in the centre, who were fighting the 'Whitecoats' of the Marquis of Newcastle. Cromwell attacked on the flank; the Whitecoats were all massacred. As the sun sank behind the Moor the last of the Royalists fled, and the battle was won. After this York surrendered, and the north of England was lost to Charles. It was then that Rupert bestowed on his conqueror the nickname of 'Ironsides', a name which was afterwards applied to the Roundhead soldiers as well as to their general.

Elsewhere the King's prospects were brighter. In Scotland the Marquis of Montrose raised a force of Highlanders to fight for the Royalist cause. In England a Royalist force, led by the King in person, surrounded and routed an army under Essex at Lostwithiel in Cornwall. Essex managed to escape by sea, but most of his army surrendered.

Essex was discredited after this adventure; Manchester, who commanded the Parliamentary forces, was reckoned to be half-hearted; Hampden and Pym were dead; it became obvious that a change of command was necessary. Parliament then agreed to pass the Self-Denying Ordinance (December 1644) by virtue of which all members of Parliament had to lay down their military commands. But the Roundheads wanted Cromwell, and after an interval of forty days he was appointed Lieutenant-General of Horse. The chief command was given to Sir Thomas Fairfax, who was not a member of Parliament, and who had already distinguished himself in the fighting in his native Yorkshire, and Cromwell was second in command.

The Self-Denying Ordinance 1644

Fairfax and Cromwell now set about re-organizing their army on the lines of Cromwell's Eastern Association. The New Model Army,

The New Model

as it was called, was trained during the winter of 1644-5, and formed the backbone of the Parliamentary forces; it at first numbered about 22,000 and reached a total of 80,000 in 1645. Though some of the men were pressed soldiers, many also belonged to all sorts of fanatical religious sects; but Cromwell told Parliament that he wanted good soldiers, not sound Presbyterians. The most important feature of the new army, however, was not its religious zeal, which was far from universal, but its regular pay. By now Parliament had perfected an effective financial system, based on the Excise, a sales tax levied on commodities such as beer and tobacco, and the Weekly Assessments, modelled on Ship Money and collected by County Committees. Paid from central funds, the New Model could be used as a national army, no longer bound by regional priorities as armies like that of the Eastern Association had been. Parliament also promised to give the generals complete control of its training. Thus a professional army was formed to fight for Parliament, and when it came into action the issue was not long in doubt. Charles could not emulate Parliament's achievement, since he lacked their resources. Dependent on the largesse of rich individuals, he had to allow them to dictate how troops should be used. The Royalist effort was dissipated as troops were dispersed defending the manor houses of Royalist supporters.

The New Model was ready to do its work by the summer of 1645. The King's chief army was in Northamptonshire. Here, at Naseby, Fairfax and Cromwell sought him out and gave battle (June 1645) lest he should attack the Scottish army and join forces with Montrose. Cromwell was confident of victory: 'I could not', he wrote in a letter, 'but smile out to God in praises, in assurance of victory, because God would, by things that are not, bring to naught things that are. Of which I had great assurance, and God did it.' The result justified his hopes, for the Royalists were completely routed. There was one more Royalist army left, under Goring, in Somerset. But Fairfax went down to the west and put it to flight at Langport (July 1645). Meanwhile Montrose, who had had some successes in Scotland

Battle of
Naseby 1645

during the previous year, was decisively defeated by the Covenanters at Philiphaugh, near Selkirk (September 1645).

In the campaign of 1644 (Marston Moor) Charles had lost the north; in 1645 (Naseby) he had lost the Midlands. The King had no more armies left to fight for him. The war became a series of sieges of towns and manor-houses. This stage of the struggle lasted about a year, and it was over when Oxford surrendered (June 1646). A month before Oxford fell, Charles had fled from the faithful city, and had surrendered at Newark to the Scots, who handed him over to Parliament a few months later in return for £400,000 (to cover their expenses) and then went home. Thus the First Civil War (1642-6) ended, both in England and Scotland, in a complete victory for the Parliamentary forces.

Fall of Oxford 1640

End of the war

2. Parliament, Army, and King

The war was over, and Parliament had won. What would they do with their victory? On the answer to this question the future of England depended; for a harsh use of victory would be sure to stir up trouble for the future. Unfortunately the Parliament men were no wiser than most others when, in their hour of triumph, they proceeded to deal with their beaten enemies. The Prayer Book service was forbidden by law, and 2,000 Anglican clergy were expelled from their livings. Having got rid of Laud, who had been put to death the year before, and, as they hoped, destroyed his Church system, Parliament turned to the Cavalier landowners. All who had fought for or helped the King were forced to pay huge fines varying from a sixth to a half of their estates. This crushing blow embittered the Royalist squires beyond hope of reconciliation. The work of this year (1646) laid the foundation of that alliance between Cavalier squire and Anglican parson which was to last for centuries. And when the Royalists returned to power under Charles II, they treated the Puritans no less harshly than the Puritans had treated them.

Victory

Crushing the Royalists

The Parliamentarians, however, were by no means united. At Westminster there was a Presbyterian majority, and, in accordance with their promise to the Scots, they set up a Presbyterian Church system by Act of Parliament. But outside Parliament, especially in the New Model army, there were many Puritan sects other than Presbyterian. Some of these sects dated from Elizabeth's day, but of late years, especially during the war, their numbers had greatly increased. The most important were the Independents and the Baptists. The Independents believed that every congregation of Christian men, even if limited to one village, should rule itself. Such freedom did not suit the Presbyterians, who were just as rigid and narrow in their views as Laud had been in his. They insisted, just as he had done, on having one uniform type of religion in England. So they passed Bills through Parliament to suppress all other sects (1646). It would have been well for them had they listened to some wise words that John Milton had recently written: 'A little generous prudence, a little forbearance of one another, and some grain of charity, might win all … into one brotherly search after truth.'

The
Independents

Milton

Not content with dashing the Independent and Baptist soldiers' hopes of religious toleration, Parliament decided to dismiss the New Model with only 8 weeks arrears of pay and with no guarantees against prosecution for what the soldiers had done to individuals during the fighting. The soldiers refused to be disbanded on these unfair terms and remained in camp, ready to mutiny. The Parliamentary leaders began to consider raising troops, apart from the New Model, to coerce the rebels in that force. Charles had been confined at Holmby House, in Lincolnshire, after the Scots had handed him over to Parliament. In June 1647 the situation was transformed by a junior New Model officer, Cornet Joyce, who with 500 men went to Holmby to seize the King. As a result, the Army leaders became major participants in the negotiations with the King designed to settle the issues that had led to civil war between him and many of his people. 'Where is your warrant?' asked the King, when

Parliament
versus Army

Cornet Joyce
1647

Joyce appeared to take him away. 'Here,' replied Joyce, pointing to his men. 'It is as fair a commission,' replied Charles, 'and as well written as I have seen in my life.' They brought him to Hampton Court, where Fairfax and Cromwell had already taken up their quarters (May 1647). Shortly after this the army marched into London, and compelled eleven leading members of Parliament to retire. After this ominous display of their power they withdrew to Bedford. They had now staked their claim to be no *mere mercenary Army*, but upholders of the public interest and the nation's freedom against corrupt and self-interested MPs.

That summer Cromwell and his son-in-law, Ireton, placed a treaty before the King called the 'Heads of the Proposals'. By this treaty Charles was to be restored to the headship of the government, the Long Parliament was at last to be dissolved and the King might even have bishops again, though there was to be freedom of worship for all the Protestant sects. Charles pretended to consider the scheme for a while, but he was encouraged to hope that he could do better by the divisions among his former opponents. In November, he suddenly escaped from Hampton Court and fled to Carisbrooke Castle, in the Isle of Wight, where he was made a prisoner. Charles once more determined to put his fate to the hazard of war, and now, at the end of 1647, he spent his time in prison in secretly arranging an alliance with the Scots, to whom he promised to establish Presbyterianism, in England. The Scots were by now prepared to support the King against the Army, owing to the failure of their scheme for enforcing Presbyterianism in England, which the Army had opposed and prevented. The Scots agreed to invade England once more and to destroy Cromwell and the New Model. It was a dangerous game that Charles was playing, for if the Scots failed him he need expect no mercy from the Ironsides. The various negotiations of 1646-8 had failed, and when Cromwell met the Army chiefs at Windsor the blame for the renewal of war was laid upon the King, and the soldiers resolved, 'if ever the Lord should bring them back again in peace, to

Heads of the Proposals 1647

Charles finds allies

57

Second Civil War

call Charles Stuart, that man of blood, to an account for the blood he had shed'.

In this spirit the Second Civil War now began. The Scots were supported by a reaction against Parliament and the Army in England. The people were paying vastly higher taxes than Charles I had ever thought of levying and in many cases the County Committees which ran local government were accused of having destroyed local liberties. Hence revolts broke out in Kent, in Essex and in South Wales. But makeshift forces in these places were no match for what may now have been the most formidable army in Europe, the New Model. While Fairfax besieged and captured the town of Colchester, Cromwell marched north to meet the Scots, put their horsemen to

Battle of Preston 1648

flight in a running fight near Preston (August 1648) and captured all their infantry. A far more bitter spirit had by this time crept into the struggle. Both Cromwell's captives in Lancashire and the defenders of Colchester were shipped off in batches to Barbados.

After Cromwell's victory, the Ironsides were masters of the situation, and there was no more fighting. On returning to London he at once turned on the Presbyterians, who had lately been so powerful in Parliament and who had begun negotiating once more with Charles I. In December he sent Colonel Pride and his musketeers to the door of the House of Commons to prevent 96 MPs who were unfriendly to the Army from entering, and to carry off 47

Pride's Purge 1648

more to prison, and this the soldiers did. After Pride's Purge, as it was called, yet more MPs stayed away in protest and generally fewer than 100 members remained to form the 'Rump' of what had been the Commons of the Long Parliament. The sword had conquered.

One thing now remained to be done, and that was to settle accounts with the King. Cromwell had decided on his death. It was Charles, he considered, who was responsible for bringing so much bloodshed on England. If the King could be forgiven for his part in the First Civil War, he certainly could not be forgiven for causing the outbreak of the Second. He seemed to Cromwell deliberately to have rejected the clear verdict of God against him expressed in his defeat in the First Civil War. And as long as Charles remained alive, Cromwell thought, and no doubt rightly thought, he would never cease to plot with Scots or Irish or French. It was useless to rely on his word, for it could not be trusted.

It was decided to put Charles through a form of trial. The Commons passed a Bill saying that it was treason for the King to levy war upon his Parliament. The Lords, of whom there were now only about a dozen left, threw out the Bill; whereupon the Commons, resolving that 'the people are, under God, the original of all just power', proceeded to act on their own authority. The next day they passed an Act (as they called it) setting up a Commission of 135 members to try the King, and declaring that Charles had endeavoured to subvert the ancient and fundamental laws and liberties of this nation, and in their place to introduce an arbitrary and tyrannical government', and that he had pursued this aim 'with fire and sword' and by 'a cruel war'. This claim to uphold the fundamental laws was undermined by their having to proceed against the King by means of a court entirely unknown to the law and hence incapable of legally trying anyone, never mind the King.

The actual trial, at which John Bradshaw, a Puritan lawyer, presided, was a tragic farce. The charge of treason could not, of course, legally be brought against the King. But Charles questioned the legality of the court in vain, and in vain protested his innocence of any 'crime' against his people. Bradshaw bullied the monarch, and finally refused to allow him to speak. He was found guilty and sentenced to death, and he was executed in front of his own palace at Whitehall on 30 January 1649.

Trial of Charles I

Execution of Charles I 1649

Charles went nobly to his death. In Andrew Marvell's words,

> He nothing common did or mean
> Upon that memorable scene,

and his proud and fearless bearing made a great impression on the multitude. A dreadful groan burst from them as the bleeding head was held up. Charles had already proclaimed himself a martyr for the Church of England and the liberties of Englishmen. Soon after his death a book called *Eikon Basilike* began to circulate. It purported to be the King's reflections, meditations and prayers during his troubles. The comparison with Christ during his Passion was meant to be irresistible. Partly thanks to this book, Charles I proved far more successful as a martyr than he had ever been as a ruler.

3. The Commonwealth

(i) *The Royalist and Dutch Wars.*

After the King's death, it was declared that the people were, under God, the origin of all just power and that England was a Commonwealth. The new government, which was set up in 1649, consisted of a Council of State and the Parliament. It was just over eight years since the Long Parliament had met, but the 'Rump' that was now left of it numbered around 80 members. The Cavalier members did not sit; the Presbyterians had been expelled by Pride's Purge. In February 1649 the House of Lords, reduced already to a tiny remnant, was declared to be 'useless and dangerous' and was abolished.

The Rump and the Council

The new Council of State contained 41 members, of whom at least 30 were Members of Parliament. These 30 men, since they were in a majority in both Council and Parliament, controlled the government, and they clung to power for four years. The Army, however, was the real master of the situation. Meanwhile Fairfax, who disapproved of the execution of Charles, retired into private life. Cromwell led his men to further victories.

Disruption of the Empire

The Roundhead victory in 1648, followed by the killing of the King, had caused a revulsion of feeling against the Puritans. It had also caused a disruption of the infant British empire. Scotland refused to recognize the new regime, and prepared to welcome Charles II from Holland; the Earl of Ormonde held Ireland in the name of the same prince. Rupert, with a Royalist fleet, including some revolted ships of the Navy, held the Channel and Scilly Isles and threatened the English coasts. Across the Atlantic, Virginia had declared for King Charles, an example which was followed by several West Indian islands.

Cromwell now had all these problems to deal with, and he began with Ireland. He landed at Dublin (August 1649), and remained in the country about nine months during which he stormed Drogheda and Wexford, massacred the garrisons and terrorized the whole population. Cromwell's conquest of Ireland was the most complete and thorough of the English conquests of that unfortunate country. The war there was prosecuted with a savagery rarely seen in the civil wars in Britain. Cromwell was anxious to finish resistance quickly before the late King's son could exploit it, but he also possessed the general 17th century English racial contempt for the Irish.

Cromwell in Ireland 1649-50

Having, as he distinctly stated, performed 'God's work' in crushing 'these barbarous wretches', Cromwell left Ireland in May 1650. In the same month the young Charles II, then aged twenty, landed in Scotland, and was welcomed in the land of his fathers. He swore to accept the National Covenant, and was crowned King at Scone. But in accepting the help of the Covenanters Charles had to agree to throw over Montrose and his Highlanders, who were mostly Catholics. Montrose was captured by his enemies, the Covenanters, and hanged at Edinburgh. Betrayed by the cause he had fought for, and insulted to the last by his foes, Montrose died a hero. Meanwhile Cromwell set out for the north. By September his army was half starving, and it might have fared ill with the Ironsides but for the rashness of David Leslie, the Scottish general. Cromwell's army lay at Dunbar, while Leslie occupied a good position on the hills above. But in the early morning of 3 September 1650, Leslie foolishly descended to the level ground, and the Ironsides attacked him before he could get his men into proper order. 'Let God arise and let His

Charles II in Scotland

Battle of Dunbar 3 Sept. 1650

CHARLES II (1630-1685, REIGN: [SCOTLAND 1649-1651] 1660-1685)
(Portrait, c. 1675, Peter Lely.)

enemies be scattered,' was Cromwell's watchword, as the sun rose above the morning mists. 'Like as the mist vanisheth, so shalt Thou drive them away.' The Scottish horse was broken first, and then the infantry which tried to come to its rescue. Ten thousand prisoners were taken, and next day Edinburgh was occupied. Leslie escaped without an army.

The following year the Scots raised another army, and decided to invade England while the Ironsides were still in possession of Scotland. There was a race through England as Cromwell followed them southwards. The two armies met in the streets of Worcester on the anniversary of Dunbar (3 September 1651), and Cromwell was again completely victorious. Few Scots escaped the slaughter of that day and the man-hunt which followed it. Among the survivors was Prince Charles, who, after being secretly sheltered by various Cavalier families, mostly Catholic, at last managed, after many hair-breadth escapes, to reach Brighton and sail for France. There were a few more Royalist risings, but none on so large a scale. Scotland was conquered, and for the next nine years it was governed by General Monk.

Battle of Worcester 3 Sept. 1651

Worcester was Cromwell's 'crowning mercy'. But the triumph of the Ironsides would have been incomplete without the work of the Navy. The Royalist fleet was still at large, preying upon English shipping, while French privateers attacked English sailors in the Channel. The republican government had not a friend in Europe, and, unless it asserted itself, it must soon collapse. The republican rulers realized that the very existence of the new state depended upon a strong navy. They acted with resolution, and put the affairs of the navy in the hands of a committee under the able Sir Henry Vane. In two years (1649-51) the navy was doubled in size – an increase of 40 to 80 ships; and during the eleven years of the Republic 207 new ships were built or acquired.

The Rebublican Navy

The command of the republican fleet was given to Robert Blake – a fortunate choice. Blake was the only leader of the time whose genius compared with Cromwell's. He was a native of Bridgwater in Somerset; he had spent ten years of his youth at Oxford, and then turned to the family business, which gave him some valuable experience of shipping. The Civil War found him, at forty-three (he was the same age as Cromwell), on the Parliamentary side. He distinguished himself by the stubborn defence of Taunton. But his wonderful energy and powers of organization were only shown when he undertook the task of re-uniting the empire under the republican flag.

Blake's chief enemy was Prince Rupert, who, like himself, had turned from land to sea warfare. Blake blockaded Rupert in his Irish base, Kinsale, and cleared the English and Irish Channels of Royalist ships. He followed Rupert to Portugal, and forced the King to dismiss his royal visitor. The Royalist fleet then entered the Mediterranean, and sheltered in Cartagena harbour. When the fleet left Cartagena, Blake fell upon it and drove most of the ships on the rocks (1651). For another year Rupert, with his remaining ships, lingered in Spanish and Portuguese waters. Then he sailed to the West Indies, but there lost all his ships except one. After that he gave up the struggle. Blake meanwhile had rounded off his victories by capturing the Channel Islands and the Scillies. One of his captains, Sir George Ayscue, secured the submission of the English West Indies and of Virginia (1652). The republican Navy was thus victorious on all the seas on which it had sailed – the Channel, the Mediterranean, and the Atlantic (1649-52). It was a great and perhaps unexpected triumph.

Defeat of Rupert's Fleet 1649-52

Eighty years had passed since Holland under William the Silent had revolted against Spain, which formally acknowledged the independence of the Dutch Republic in 1648. During that time the Dutch had become a great trading and naval power, wresting the command of the sea from Spain. They had captured various Portuguese trading-stations in the East Indies, including the Spice Islands which they held until the Second World War; and they had formed a settlement at the Cape of Good Hope guarding the route to the east. It was in the east that they first came into collision with English traders, whom they treated with contempt and violence. A number of English traders were massacred at Amboyna in 1623 and the English were driven from the East Indian islands, though not from India itself. Year by year the fleets of the Dutch East India Company brought back rich cargoes to Amsterdam, rivalling those which sailed to Cadiz from the Spanish Main.

Dutch naval supremacy

Their victory over their rivals, together with their great prosperity, caused the Dutch to regard themselves as masters of the seas. In the North Sea they fought the English sailors, and drove them from the fisheries. The Commonwealth Parliament insisted that this treatment should cease, and they added the somewhat insolent demand that the Dutch should salute the English flag in the Narrow Seas (the Channel and southern North Sea), which they called 'English waters'. English feeling was further outraged when the ambassador at The Hague was murdered in his hotel. Another cause of friction was that English sailors, who were at this time fighting the French privateers in the Channel, demanded the right to search neutral vessels which might be carrying goods to France. Acting on this excuse, English sailors, who hated their Dutch rivals, stopped and searched as many Dutch ships as they could.

Anglo-Dutch rivlry

Especially after the trade depression of 1648-51, it seemed essential to the Commonwealth government to protect and further English trade against the all-powerful Dutch. Parliament therefore passed a Navigation Act (1651), as previous Parliaments from the days of Richard II had done. This Act laid down that goods imported from America, Asia, and Africa into England, Ireland, or the Colonies must be carried in ships owned by Englishmen and manned by crews more than half English, and that goods imported from Europe must be carried in English ships or in the ships of the country from which the goods came. The difference between this Act and earlier ones was that the government had the determination and financial and naval resources to enforce it. The Dutch merchants, who at that time carried a large proportion of the goods imported into England, protested at this blow to their trade, and negotiations between the two countries were opened. But before any agreement could be reached, fighting broke out between the rival sailors. Blake met a Dutch fleet under Tromp off the coast of Kent, shots were exchanged, and the war began.

Navigation Act 1651

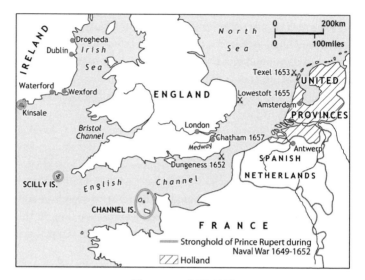

NAVAL WARS (1649-1667)

'The English are about to attack a mountain of gold; we a mountain of iron,' remarked one of the Dutch envoys. There was much truth in this: the Dutch had everything to lose, England little. Holland was a rich, thickly populated country, and the very existence of her teeming cities depended on the maintenance of her sea-borne trade. England, on the other hand, was still an agricultural country, and so could not be starved into submission. Besides this the Dutch suffered from the great disadvantage that their trading fleet must either pass through the English Channel or go round the British Isles and across the North Sea. In either case the fleet, unless heavily protected, must fall a prey to the English.

In actual fighting-power there was not much to choose between the two navies. The English attacked the Dutch merchant fleets, and the Dutch admirals – Tromp, de Witt, and de Ruyter – therefore used their warships as convoys for their merchantmen. Tromp defeated Blake off Dungeness (1652) and successfully convoyed a great fleet of 450 merchantmen down the Channel. But next summer the two fighting fleets met off the coast of Suffolk, and this time Blake gained the victory. The Dutch retired to their ports, and a blockade of their coast followed. There was one more naval battle off Texel, in which Tromp was killed and both fleets suffered severely. But by now (1653) the Dutch cities were starving, and their government was ready to come to terms. Peace was made in the following year, 1654, by Cromwell, who had taken over the government and wanted to end English isolation in Europe by offering the Dutch a generous peace. The Dutch conceded English supremacy in the Narrow Seas, and withdrew their objections to the Navigation Act.

First Dutch War 1652-4

The war, however, had been very costly, although the English had captured 1,500 prizes, double the number of their existing merchant fleet. But the cost of the Navy during the war was £1,000,000 a year – more than the total revenue of Charles I. The money was raised largely from heavy taxation of Cavalier estates and from the sale of land formerly belonging to the bishops.

Cost of the War

(ii) *The End of the Rump.*

Before the Dutch war was over a change took place in the government of England. The Army had demanded the dismissal of the Rump and the election of a new Parliament. But the Rump was not keen to give up its power and it was hard to devise a Parliament that would not prove hostile to the republican constitution. Yet as the months went by, the Rump did very little to bring about the godly reformation which many in the Army desired. It abolished the use of Norman French in the law courts, but nothing else was done to speed up or to make less expensive the processes of the law, and its religious policy was indecisive and incoherent. On 20th April 1653 Cromwell finally lost patience with them. He had sat down in his place and listened to the debate. But finally he rose and addressed the House. 'Your hour is come,' he told the members, 'the Lord hath done with

Cromwell and the Rump

THE END OF THE RUMP
Cromwell drives out the members: 'Be gone you rogues, you have sate long enough.'
(From a contemporary Dutch cartoon)

you.' Shouts of protest were raised, but the general strode into the middle of the House crying: 'I will put an end to your prating. You should give place to better men. You are no Parliament.' He then signed to his soldiers, who entered and cleared the House. Cromwell lifted the Mace from the table. 'What shall we do with this bauble?' he cried; 'take it away!' Next day someone posted a placard on the locked door of the House: 'This House is to be let, but unfurnished!'

The Rump driven out April 1653

It was an unhappy business, and Cromwell felt it to be so. 'I have sought the Lord day and night that He would rather slay me than put upon me the doing of this work. But [he told the members] it is you who have forced me to this.' Providence and necessity had compelled him to act as he did, Cromwell believed. The Rump had been far too anxious to cling to power, and had done far too little to justify their retention of it. There was no protest against their expulsion – 'not a dog barked', said Cromwell. In the streets of London people celebrated the dismissal of the Rump by roasting rump steaks. But it meant that with King, Lords and now Commons all abolished, the search for a settlement of England's constitution had to begin from scratch.

Cromwell had apparently not decided what to do next. As a temporary expedient, he chose to put a nominated Parliament in place of the Rump. Those who sat in it were chosen in part from the Puritan sects – men 'faithful, fearing God, and hating covetousness', but Cromwell and the senior officers were too cautious to select many who were not gentlemen certain to defend the existing social order. At first the Lord General was enthusiastic about the new Parliament, and thought that the Rule of the Saints had come at last. But this Barebones Parliament – as it was called from the name of one of its members, Praise-God Barebone – disappointed him. Various revolutionary schemes, such as the abolition of Church tithes and the introduction of the Law of Moses in place of the Common Law, were proposed. Cromwell, who was at heart a conservative, grew alarmed. 'Nothing was in the hearts of these men,' he remarked, 'but overturn, overturn.' The more moderate members insisted on bringing the Parliament to an end in December 1653, and carried a vote 'that it is requisite to deliver up to the Lord General the powers we received from him'.

Barebones Parliament 1653

The Army officers now decided to make a new scheme of government. They drew up the 'Instrument of Government', which set up what was virtually a new monarchy, with Cromwell as monarch. He was to take the title, not of King, but of Lord Protector. Power was divided – on paper – between the Protector, the Council, and a Parliament. But the real power lay with the Protector, backed by the Army. The *Parliamentary* Republic had failed; the *Presidential* Republic, under a 'Protector' was now to be tried.

The Instrument of Government 1653

4. The Protectorate of Oliver Cromwell

Cromwell's position was unique in English history. He himself firmly believed that he had been specially called by Divine Providence to perform a great task. There was no hypocrisy in this, nor in Cromwell's habit of constantly referring to the divine guidance to justify his actions. The language of the Puritans may not suit modern taste, but it was sincere enough. Cromwell addressed himself to his task in a suitable spirit without pride, but without weakness. He once compared himself to 'a good constable, set to keep the peace of the parish'. His enemies might object that he brought not peace but a sword. For it was the sword that had made Cromwell what he now was, the dictator of England, and, try as he might, he could never lay the sword aside.

The Good Constable

A staunch republican, Ludlow by name, once told Cromwell that, under his government, England had lost what the Puritan soldiers had fought for – government by the consent of the people. 'I am as much for government by consent as any man,' he answered, 'but where will you find that consent?' This was the crux of the whole matter. For not only was at least half of England Royalist, but the non-Royalists themselves were by now so hopelessly divided that to reach any kind of agreement was impossible. Another critic told Cromwell that nine out of ten men in England were against him. 'Very well,' he replied, but what if I should disarm the nine, and put a sword in the tenth man's hands? Would not that do the business?' It would, and as long as Oliver lived, it did. When his first Parliament asked him to give up to them the control of the army, he refused. He refused because he could trust no one but himself to maintain order; and the events which followed his death showed that he was right.

Rule of the sword

First Protectorate Parliament 1654-5

The first Parliament of the Protectorate sat for four months (September 1654-January 1655). Oliver and his officers prevented 100 duly elected members from sitting because they refused to swear to uphold the constitution under the Instrument of Government). In spite of this high-handed action – which makes the arbitrary acts of Charles I look small by comparison – the Parliament still caused him much trouble for the remaining members discussed the Protector's powers and proposed to reduce the Army and the taxes which paid for it. As soon as he could Oliver angrily dismissed the Parliament (January 1655).

He then tried the experiment of dividing England into twelve districts, each ruled by one of his Major-Generals (1655). This military rule was necessary, Cromwell thought, because of the unquiet state of the country. There had been Royalist risings in Scotland and elsewhere. The Royalist plotters were joined by extreme republicans – the Levellers and the Fifth Monarchy Men,[5] who detested the Protector's rule. The officers suppressed these risings with a firm hand. The Major-Generals, besides putting down rebellion, set up a kind of censorship of morals, and tried to regulate the conduct of private persons in a manner odious to the gentry, who resented these rivals for the control of local government. Nothing that Oliver did was so unpopular as this. His continued rule depended on his maintaining support from both the Army and the gentry. The rule of the Major-Generals alienated the latter.

The Major-Generals 1655

Next year Oliver gave up the experiment and called another Parliament (September 1656). As before, the Protector and the Council excluded 100 members whom they thought would oppose the Government. It was this Parliament which presented The Humble Petition and Advice (1657) praying Oliver to assume the crown. He considered doing so, not that he wanted the title of King

Second Parliament 1656-8

Humble Petition and Advice 1657

---

[5] The Levellers wanted many more men to be allowed the vote, but did not wish, as their enemies alleged, to abolish distinctions of rank. The Fifth Monarchy Men believed that the world had been ruled (as stated in the Bible) by four monarchies – Assyria, Persia, Macedonia, and Rome. The last of these having fallen, it was time for the Fifth Monarchy – the reign of Christ and His Saints on earth.

– a 'feather in a hat' he called it – but because he thought the change might enhance his chance of reaching a settlement. But the army officers, staunch republicans, would have none of it, and he therefore refused the title. He was, however, installed again as Protector with larger powers, including the right to nominate his successor, and consented to create a new Other House, chosen from the existing Commons.

But the new Parliament worked no better than the old. The Commons again criticized the constitution, and Oliver, thinking they were merely throwing the country back into confusion, dissolved the Parliament in anger (February 1658): 'I think it high time,' he told them, 'that an end be put to your sitting, and I do dissolve this Parliament. And let God judge between you and me.' 'Amen,' replied the defiant members. The Protector never met another Parliament. King and Church, Lords and Commons, had all gone; the army alone remained.

It will have been noted that many of Oliver's acts were just as arbitrary and despotic as those of Charles I. But this was not all. Cromwell did not hesitate to tax the people without consent of

Despotic Acts

Parliament, and to throw men into prison without any form of trial. Necessity was Cromwell's plea. 'If nothing should be done,' said he, 'but what is according to law, the throat of the nation might be cut while we send for someone to make a law.' Charles I had justified his actions in levying Ship Money or arresting subversive MPs such as Eliot on exactly the same grounds.

Parliamentary Reform

But in spite of the obvious criticism that Oliver's government was just as despotic as that of the Stuarts which it had supplanted, it had carried out useful reforms. The reform of Parliament, introduced under the Protectorate, had much to recommend it. The Protectorate Parliaments included members from England, Scotland, and Ireland, thus giving to the British Isles a real measure of unity for the first time in history. Besides this the borough members were reduced from 430 to 139, and insignificant towns lost their seats to the larger and more prosperous towns. This desirable reform was swept away by Charles II: and the old decaying boroughs retained their members till the great Reform Bill of the nineteenth century.

The Protector, like the whole-hearted Puritan he was, was bent on a reform of the national morals and manners: He issued ordinances against drunkenness, duelling, cock-fighting, bear-baiting, and even horse-racing. He was himself a keen rider and hunter and he stopped horse-racing only because it gave opportunities for gatherings of Cavaliers and other subversive groups. The Long Parliament had already closed the theatres, and Cromwell himself tried to enforce the Puritan Sabbath by law. His second Parliament even passed an Act to punish persons 'vainly and profanely walking' on the Sabbath Day. All this interference with the daily lives of the people made godly reformation very unpopular. But though, in some respects, Puritan views were narrow, the aim was high. 'The mind is the man,' said Oliver; 'if that be kept pure, the man signifies somewhat; if not, I would very fain see what difference there is between him and a beast.' It cannot be doubted that there was much evil-living and drunkenness in seventeenth-century England. But Oliver, strict as he was, never dreamt of such a thing as prohibiting the sale of drink because some men might get drunk. 'It will be found,' he wisely said, 'an unjust and unwise jealousy to deprive a man of his natural liberty upon a supposition that he may abuse it. When he doth abuse it, judge.'

Puritan Reforms

In religious matters Oliver's Government has been described as the most tolerant set up in England up to that time. The State Church admitted clergy of the three main Puritan sects – Presbyterian, Independent, and Baptist – the 'three sorts of godly men'. But in practice nearly all the Puritan sects were tolerated, and even the Anglicans who wished to use the Prayer Book were not as heavily persecuted as they had been under the Long Parliament. Cromwell's notions of religious freedom, indeed, went far beyond those of his contemporaries. Public opinion would not permit of his tolerating Roman Catholics, yet he wrote to Cardinal Mazarin, the effective

Question of Toleration

ruler of France, that he had 'plucked many [Catholics] out of the fire – the raging fire of persecution'. He added that it was his purpose 'as soon as I can remove impediments, and some weights that press me down' to make further progress towards fuller toleration. But he was never able to do so.

The Protector allowed some Jewish traders to come and settle in England – the first who had been permitted to do so since the expulsion of the Jews by Edward I. He also checked the Puritan fury against the Society of Friends, known as the Quakers. The Friends were founded in 1647 by George Fox. This remarkable man was gifted with an almost supernatural power of convincing others by his preaching – a power which may be likened to that of some of the medieval saints. Fox believed that the only form of force which was worth anything was the force of example; his followers were exhorted to embrace martyrdom if need be, but never to resist. The Quakers were the first men in modern England to preach the essential wickedness of all war. In later times the good works done by them in acts of public and private charity have compelled the admiration of all classes. But in their early days they provoked fierce hatred by their habit of entering churches during a service and denouncing the preacher in the presence of the congregation. They were often brutally attacked, though Cromwell admired their sincerity, and often protected them from violence. He released many Quakers from prison. But he could not prevent Parliament from causing James Naylor, a Friend, to be pilloried, whipped, branded, and imprisoned for blasphemy. But to stay the force of religious bigotry was beyond even Cromwell's powers.

George Fox and the Quakers

In foreign policy Oliver took a bold line. It was his dearest wish to see a league of Protestant Powers in Europe, with England at the head. The crowned heads of Europe had at first looked with equal scorn and hatred on the regicide government of England, but Blake's victories over Rupert and the Dutch made them change their tone. The usurper who had expelled the Stuarts was soon more respected

Foreign Policy

in Europe than the Stuarts had ever been. Cromwell was indignant at the news that the Duke of Savoy had massacred a large number of his Protestant subjects in Piedmont.

Massacre in Piedmont

> Avenge, O Lord, Thy slaughtered saints, whose bones
> Lie scattered on the Alpine mountains cold

wrote Milton in a famous sonnet. Oliver's protests to the government of Cardinal Mazarin brought pressure to bear on the Duke, and the persecution was stopped.

Cromwell revived the Elizabethan tradition of hostility to Spain, a country which he regarded as the arch-enemy of the Protestant faith. He demanded that English traders should not be molested by the Inquisition, and that the West Indian trade should be thrown open. This, remarked the Spanish ambassador, was to ask 'for his master's two eyes'. Without waiting to declare war, Cromwell sent an expedition under Admiral Penn and General Venables to the West Indies, with instructions to attack Hispaniola (1655). Though this attack failed, the English took Jamaica, which became a British possession for 300 years. Blake also carried out a blockade of the Spanish coast, and destroyed the Spanish treasure fleet at Santa Cruz. This was the great admiral's last exploit, for he died as his ship entered Plymouth Sound (1657). In the story of the English navy Blake ranks with Drake and Nelson.

Spanish War

Jamaica 1655

Meanwhile Oliver had made an alliance with France, then ruled by Cardinal Mazarin in the name of the young Louis XIV. An Anglo-French army attacked the town of Dunkirk, in the Spanish Netherlands. The brothers of Charles II serving in the Spanish army, witnessed the Ironside attack, and they could not but admire the valour and discipline of their countrymen as that famous army put the troops of Spain to flight at the battle of the Dunes. Dunkirk was surrendered to Louis, who handed it over to Oliver. This was the last victory of the Ironsides (1658).

Dunkirk 1658

The news of Dunkirk came to cheer a sick man. Oliver himself was soon to lay aside both sword and sceptre. The loss of a favourite daughter preyed on his failing health and spirits; he was seized with an ague and sank rapidly. September 3rd dawned, the day of victories, the day of Dunbar and Worcester. Cromwell did not live to see its close; before the evening that mighty, troubled spirit was at rest.

Death of
Cromwell
3 Sept. 1658

Cromwell failed to solve the Stuart problem of how to combine parliamentary institutions with personal rule. The republicans were so divided amongst themselves that Oliver found it impossible to work with his Parliaments, and he had to fall back upon military force. He was the victim of 'Cruel Necessity' – words said to have been uttered by Cromwell over the dead body of Charles I. His religious policy pleased only some few upholders of toleration. He crushed Catholic Ireland; he pacified Presbyterian Scotland; above all, he gave England peace after civil war. And, wrote Clarendon, 'Cromwell's greatness at home was a mere shadow of his greatness abroad'.

5. The End of the Republic

The Humble Petition and Advice had given Oliver Cromwell the right of naming his successor. He had named his eldest son, Richard Cromwell. Richard had had little connection with his father's regime and, doubtless for this reason, at once achieved a popularity which the dead Protector had never enjoyed. He was installed in his father's place without question.

Richard
Cromwell

In January 1659 the new Protector summoned a Parliament to help resolve the regime's urgent financial problems. Parliament at once proceeded to quarrel with the Army officers. The latter wished to make General Fleetwood head of the army instead of the Protector. Richard at first sided with Parliament, but was not strong enough to brave the officers, who presented a united front, and at their bidding he dissolved his Parliament (April). Next month, promising to pay the Army its arrears of pay, the Rump reassembled at Westminster to assume the government, and Richard gave up his authority. Such was the end of the fiasco of the rule of 'Tumbledown Dick' as he was called.

End of Richard's rule 1659

For the remainder of the year 1659 the country was dangerously near anarchy. The Rump soon quarrelled with the generals and tried to get rid of several, including Lambert, probably the most powerful. In October General Lambert prevented by force the entry of the members of the Rump to Westminster, and it seemed as if the naked sword must rule supreme. Yet the sword could rule only so long as those who wielded it remained united. In 1659 one of the generals broke ranks. He was General Monk, the Army commander in Scotland. Monk saw that a settlement must be made, and determined to make it – but he told no one what his exact intentions were, probably because they evolved as events developed. Monk thoroughly purged his army and secured its loyalty by generous pay from Scottish taxes. Declaring his allegiance to the Rump, he marched his army south and occupied London (February 1660) at the invitation of a restored Rump. Massive agitation for a free Parliament led Monk to insist on the Long Parliament being restored, including the Presbyterian members expelled by Pride's Purge in 1648. There was, however, a general demand for a new Parliament, and so the old Long Parliament, first called by Charles I in 1640, voted the heavy taxes needed to pay the army and then at last dissolved itself in March 1660.

General Monk

End of the Long Parliament 1660

The elections were held amid great excitement and the new Parliament – known as the Convention, because it was not summoned by a king – assembled. It at once voted for the return of the old constitution – King, Lords and Commons, and the old laws. Charles II, already in communication with Monk, signed the Declaration of Breda, by which he agreed to return and assume the crown.

The Convention 1660

Charles II landed at Dover among scenes of tremendous enthusiasm, and on the 29th of May, his thirtieth birthday, he rode

Return of Charles II May 1660

from Rochester to London, through miles of cheering multitudes. It took him seven hours to pass through the crowded streets of the capital to Whitehall. He reached the palace at last, and entered the Banqueting Hall outside which his father's scaffold had once stood. The old times had come back with an almost universal chorus of 'God Save the King'. The Puritan Revolution had failed, and it had failed mainly for three reasons. First, the people were tired of Puritan discipline, which attempted to make men good by force. Secondly, the gentry of England were tired of the rule of soldiers and were determined, whatever else might happen, never again to submit to a military dictatorship. Lastly, the gentry were tired of a revolution, which had done far more to endanger their rule than any King ever had, and looked, as people will look, to a return of 'the good old times'.

End of the Puritan Experiment

If the Puritan Revolution had left its mark on England, it was as an example of what must in future be avoided. In many ways, Charles I had triumphed from beyond the grave. He had fought and manoeuvred for the unconditional restoration of his monarchy and in the end his son was restored without conditions. The Puritan enemies of Charles and Archbishop Laud were discredited and rule of the Church by bishops was never again challenged. Opposition to future Stuart monarchs would be inhibited by the paramount need to prevent a new civil war. There was a good chance that Charles II might become a more powerful King than his forebears.

III

Charles II and James II

1. The Restoration

(i) *In England.*

THE man who was welcomed back to England in 1660 with such
enthusiasm was hardly a typical Englishman. His long residence
abroad had made Charles II almost a foreigner in appearance and
manners; his mother had been a French princess.[6] Nevertheless
Charles liked England, and it was his fixed determination never again
to leave her shores – never, as he put it, to go on his travels again. This
was a guiding principle – almost the only principle – of his life.
Charles was a good-looking, easy-going man, with a fund of wit and
good humour which endeared him to his companions. His faults
were those of the Cavaliers who crowded to his court, and whose lives
expressed the reaction against Puritan severity. The gaiety and the
scandals of his court, where satin coats and long flowing wigs now

Charles II
1660-85

---

[6] Table showing the connection between the House of Stuart and the French Royal
House and the House of Orange.

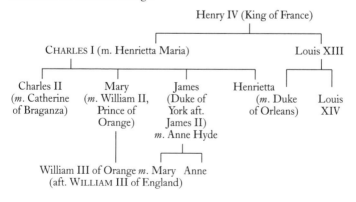

became fashionable, helped to degrade the reputation of the monarchy, as scurrilous verse circulated describing Charles' series of affairs with his mistresses. The King was easily bored by administrative details and showed nothing of the professionalism of his cousin, King Louis XIV of France, but was always ready to laugh at the latest jest.

So much appeared on the surface; but Charles had other capabilities. He was a far abler man than his father or brother, and he was capable of carrying out deep-laid schemes, which he concealed under a charming manner and an apparent contempt for business. He was also quite capable of dishonesty, and was too cynical to value a sense of honour in other people. How far his plotting and dishonesty led him will appear presently. At times he came close to alienating popular feeling, but he was too wise to do so irrevocably, as his father and brother did. A friend once summed up Charles' character in the words of a pretended epitaph:

Character of Charles II

> Here lies our sovereign lord the king,
> Whose word no man relies on,
> Who never said a foolish thing,
> Nor ever did a wise one.

'True,' replied Charles, with his ready wit, 'for my words are my own, but my acts are my ministers'.'

The first business after the King's return was to construct a ministry. Its members were chosen from the old Cavaliers who had followed the King into exile, and from the Presbyterians who had helped in his restoration. The chief minister was Edward Hyde, Earl of Clarendon, the Lord Chancellor. Clarendon had followed the House of Stuart through good fortune and through ill for twenty years. On him fell the main burden of adapting the institutions of the England of his youth to the changed circumstances of the post-Commonwealth era. For the first seven years of the reign he was,

Clarendon

after the King, the most important person in England. Clarendon's ideal was a restored Crown, working in conjunction with Parliament, and a restored Church, based on the support of the Cavaliers. Charles had not Clarendon's reverence either for Parliament or for the Church, and he had other views on both questions. But he did not interfere; he bided his time.

The Restoration of 1660 was the restoration of the King, the Lords and Commons, and the Church. Charles had been recalled by a freely elected representative body. But that fact did not prevent churchmen in particular from describing the restoration as the work of God. They began again to stress that the King ruled by divine right, and Charles emphasised the God-given nature of his authority by reviving the practice of touching for the King's evil, a skin disease thought to be magically alleviated by the royal touch. Even more than under the early Stuarts, it was taught that any resistance to the King was sinful. Yet those who restored the King intended that he should uphold the ancient laws and institutions of the country: this was to be the great difference between him and Cromwell. Hence Charles did not recover what his father had been compelled to concede in the first half of 1641, though he did regain powers to appoint ministers and control the militia, which Pym had disputed from the autumn of 1641 onwards.

The Restoration settlement was based on the Declaration of Breda, signed by the King before he left Holland. In this Charles had promised four things: first, a general pardon to all the old Roundheads concerned in the Rebellion, save such as Parliament should except; second, the payment of arrears to the Army; third, the settlement by Parliament of the land question, involving estates which had changed hands; and fourth, a 'liberty to tender consciences' in religious matters.

Declaration of Breda

The first three of these matters were dealt with by the Convention (April-December 1660); the religious question was settled later. Strangely enough, Charles himself was more mercifully inclined to old rebels than were the Lords and Commons. Eventually it was decided that the regicides, i.e. those who had actually taken part in the trial and execution of Charles I, should be marked out for vengeance. The regicides were brought to trial, and ten of them were executed. Another victim was the stern republican, Sir Henry Vane, who was not a regicide, but whom Parliament thought too dangerous to be left alive. Vane died for his principles, proud and brave to the last. Revenge was also taken on the dead. The body of Cromwell was dug up, hung in chains, and then beheaded; the remains of Bradshaw and Ireton were treated in a similar fashion. The heads were then stuck on poles over Westminster Hall.

Execution of the Regicides

The famous Ironside Army was paid off and granted immunity from prosecution for what its members had done in the years of the war and interregnum, and the soldiers retired quietly and with dignity into private life. The whole country was tired of soldiers, and no English Parliament, however devoted to the monarch, would henceforth grant him the right of keeping a standing army. Charles II had to be content with a few guards, of whom Monk's Coldstreamers were the first, three or four thousand in total.

Disbandment of Army

The land question was a great difficulty, since so many estates had changed hands since 1642. Crown and Church lands were restored unconditionally to their original owners; so too were private lands directly confiscated by the Commonwealth. But Cavaliers who had been forced, through taxation, to sell their estates had to abide their loss. The King was accused of ingratitude on this account, but it is difficult to see what else could have been done.

The Land Question

The Convention also settled the important question of finance. It was calculated that the total income of Charles I from all sources had been £900,000, but that his expenditure had exceeded that amount by £200,000. Parliament therefore granted Charles II a regular income of £1,200,000, to be raised by taxation, assuming that this would be a sufficient revenue on which to rule the country. In fact, Parliament had miscalculated both the yield of the taxes imposed and the

Finance

government's needs and in the 1660s and 1670s Charles constantly had to ask Parliament for more. Consequently, he had little freedom of manoeuvre and sought from time to time to free himself from Parliamentary control.

The Convention, which contained the Presbyterians and Cavaliers who had combined to restore the king, was dissolved at the end of 1660. The Cavalier Parliament, which assembled the following year, was of a different character. Charles, observing that the members were full of enthusiastic loyalty and mostly young men, said he would keep them till they grew beards. He kept them for eighteen years (1661-79). It was this Cavalier Parliament which settled the religious question to its own satisfaction. It was decided that the Anglican Church, with the bishops and the Prayer Book, was to be the Church of England. No concessions were made over such matters as the use of the surplice and kneeling at the sacrament. In this way Archbishop Laud won a posthumous victory and the Presbyterians, who had believed themselves secure, were undeceived. They had refused to tolerate the sects; now they found themselves treated as one of the sects, and excluded from the Church they had hoped to control.

Cavalier Parliament 1661-79

The Anglican triumph seems to have accorded with the wishes of most people of all classes. It was against the wishes of the King, who was anxious to win the support of the Nonconformists, but he found Cavalier zeal too strong for him. Clarendon, also, would have preferred a less harsh persecution of the sects than that on which Parliament insisted; but history has attached the name 'Clarendon Code' (1661-5) to the persecuting Acts passed at this period. First came the Corporation Act (1661) by which the government of town corporations was placed in the hands of Anglicans, and every holder of municipal office had to receive the Communion according to the rites of the Church of England. The following year an Act of Uniformity (1662) made the use of the Prayer Book compulsory in English churches. Two thousand Puritan ministers who refused to

Clarendon

conform were turned out of their livings.[7] The effect of these two Acts was to create the division between the Church and the Dissenters (or Nonconformists, as those who refused to conform to the Act of 1662 were called) which has endured to the present day. In practice, those who wished to have any share in the government of their town or village conformed to the Acts. The result was that for many centuries 'Church people' were the rulers of England, and the Dissenters sank in the social scale.

But the Cavalier Parliament was not content with thus thrusting the Puritans out of the Church. A Quaker Act was passed (1662) inflicting severe penalties on those who attended Quaker meetings, and no fewer than 5,000 Quakers were cast into prison, many dying on account of their sufferings. The Conventicle Act (1664) inflicted similar penalties on those who attended any Nonconformist 'conventicle', or religious meeting. It was under this Act that John Bunyan, author of *The Pilgrim's Progress*, spent twelve years in Bedford Gaol. Lastly the Five Mile Act (1665) forbade Nonconformist ministers to live, or to build chapels, in any corporate town[8] or within five miles of one.

Persecution of the Sects

The Puritan sects, though they suffered less as the years went by and Anglican fury cooled down, none the less did suffer severely. The Clarendon Code compares very unfavourably with the comparatively tolerant attitude of Cromwell. But the sects, or Nonconformist churches as we must now call them, did not disappear, but henceforth became a permanent feature of English life.

(ii) *In Scotland.*

The Restoration settlement in Scotland restored the country to the

---

[7] It should be remembered that a large proportion of the ejected ministers had obtained their livings by the ejection of their predecessors.

[8] A corporate town possessed certain municipal rights, and was governed by a corporation or town council.

position of 1633. The limits imposed since then on royal power were all removed. The full union with England established by Cromwell was ended. For example, Cromwell had set up free trade between England and Scotland: this arrangement was now overthrown, and Scotland treated as a foreign country by England, to the disadvantage of Scottish trade.

But the main trouble was religion. Charles had, in 1650, sworn to observe both the National Covenant and the Solemn League and Covenant. The former bound him to uphold the Presbyterian Kirk in Scotland, the latter to establish it in England. It was quite obvious – except to Scottish fanatics – that it was impossible for him to fulfil the second of these promises. Charles had no intention of keeping the first promise either. The King wanted a degree of conformity with his other kingdoms and he believed that he could more easily rule the Scottish Kirk through bishops than through the General Assembly of a Presbyterian Church. The Scots therefore had to accept bishops placed over their Kirk, though no attempt was made to introduce the English Prayer Book. About a third of the Scottish parish clergy were driven out of the reorganized Church.

Charles II and the Covenanters

The Earl of Lauderdale was made Secretary for Scotland, and he ruled the country for nearly twenty years. A religious persecution was carried on of all who could not be accommodated in the Church, which gradually turned many Scots into rebels. The National Covenant was denounced as illegal, Presbyterian ministers were prevented from preaching, and finally anyone who preached at a conventicle (unauthorised religious meeting) was liable to imprisonment and large fines. Rebellion came in 1679. In that year Archbishop Sharpe of St. Andrews – regarded as a turncoat Presbyterian minister – was murdered by Covenanters. This crime was followed by a serious rising in the West Highlands. Lauderdale was recalled, and replaced by the Duke of Monmouth, the eldest of the king's illegitimate sons, who led an army against the rebels, and defeated them at Bothwell Bridge (1679). Monmouth was

Lauderdale

Scottish Rebellion 1679

superseded by his uncle, James, Duke of York, the King's brother, but it was after his departure that a savage campaign of repression was mounted against the Crown's religious and political critics. This The 'Killing period is known in Scottish history as the 'Killing Time'. The Time' Covenanters were hunted like animals, shot down at sight or taken and tortured. The government in Scotland had much less limited powers than had Charles' government in England and it used them unsparingly to make itself secure.

2. The Dutch Wars of Charles II

In the seventeenth century there was little general desire for peace in Europe. Ambitious monarchs, or fighting traders and sailors, might Portuguese cause war to break out at any time. In England the French, Alliance Spaniards, and more recently the Dutch, were regarded with varying degrees of suspicion and dislike. But the new reign began with a peace move; a Portuguese alliance was established, and celebrated by the marriage of Charles II to Catherine of Braganza, sister of the King of Portugal. Catherine brought her husband a handsome dowry Bombay of £800,000, while her brother ceded Tangier and Bombay to the English King. Charles, however, soon sold Bombay to the East India Company. He also sold Dunkirk, gained from Spain by Cromwell, to Louis XIV of France for £2,000,000.

It was not long before the commercial rivalry of England and Holland in America, in Africa, and in the east led again to war. The Second Dutch War (1664-7) followed the seizure by the English of Second New Amsterdam, the Dutch colony in North America, which was Dutch War renamed New York in honour of the king's brother, the Duke of 1664-7 York. The duke and his cousin Prince Rupert were in command of the naval war while the Dutch were commanded by de Ruyter, and there were several battles, such as one off Lowestoft in 1665, in the North Sea. Expectations that the war would prove profitable were dashed, as few prizes were taken. Meanwhile England was crippled by two great disasters which befell London, the Plague and the Great Fire (1665-6). In 1667 the government was so short of money and Charles' court was so extravagant that the sailors were left unpaid and mutinied, and the fleet was laid up at Chatham. De Ruyter took advantage of this to sail up the Medway, destroy sixteen ships, and bombard Chatham dockyard; he sailed away again with the ship, the *Royal Charles*, in tow. This disgrace was keenly felt in England. 'Everyone nowadays', wrote Pepys, 'reflects upon Oliver, and commends him, what brave things he did, and made all the neighbouring princes fear him.' In the same year the Government made peace (Treaty of Breda, 1667), by which the Dutch submitted to the loss of their American colonies (New Amsterdam and New Jersey). As an offset, England gave up Surinam in South America to the Dutch.

The humiliation of the Dutch raid had made the government very unpopular. Owing largely to the ill-success of the war, Charles decided to sacrifice his faithful minister Clarendon, who had never wanted the war, but had failed to control those who did. He became the scapegoat for failure, was dismissed and then impeached by Parliament for misconducting the war (1667). The old minister fled to France, where he spent the rest of his life writing his famous *History of the Great Rebellion*. The profits from the sale of this work were afterwards used to provide a building for the University Press (also known as the Clarendon Press) at Oxford.

Charles' new ministry was known as 'the Cabal', a word meaning a secret intrigue, which happened to correspond to the initials of its five leading members – Clifford, Arlington, Buckingham, Ashley-Cooper, and Lauderdale. Arlington was the most important of these men and his first action in foreign affairs was to negotiate the Triple Alliance of 1668 between England, Holland, and Sweden against France, which had just overrun a large part of the Spanish Netherlands – 'the only good public thing that hath been done since the King came to England', wrote Pepys of the Alliance. After Clarendon's fall Charles had determined to assert himself and his object in allowing this treaty

Fall of
Clarendon
1667

to be signed seems to have been to persuade Louis XIV of France that he needed to buy an alliance with England. Charles' scheme to ally England with France was confided only to Sir Thomas Clifford, a Catholic, and then to Arlington, whom he won over to his side.

The Cabal 1667-73

The famous alliance of 1670 between Charles II and his cousin Louis XIV needs some explanation. On Louis' side the alliance was part of an extensive scheme to isolate the Dutch and then attack them. Louis, the *Grand Monarque* of French history, wished to strengthen his vulnerable northern frontier by absorbing the Spanish Netherlands. Before he could proceed with these plans, he saw that he must first destroy the power of the Dutch, and therefore break up the Anglo-Dutch alliance.

Louis XIV and Holland

On Charles' side this alliance was part of a deep-laid plot. He confided this plot only to Clifford and Arlington, and to his sister Henrietta, Duchess of Orleans, who had married Louis' brother. It was the duchess who arranged the signing of the Secret Treaty of Dover between Charles and Louis in 1670. In this Charles promised, first, in consideration of a sum of £230,000 per annum, to join in the naval attack on Holland (in spite of the Triple Alliance); and, secondly, to declare himself a Roman Catholic and then to re-establish the Catholic religion in England. In case Charles' subjects should object, Louis promised a further sum of money, to be paid in advance, and the aid of 6,000 French troops. Only a *sham* Treaty – omitting the religious clause of the Secret Treaty – was made known to Parliament or even to the members of the Cabal, except Arlington and Clifford, who were in the secret. Charles' motives in making the Secret Treaty of Dover are hard to fathom. He never took any steps to declare himself a Catholic, but perhaps the Catholic clauses were intended simply to get more money from Louis and to strengthen the friendship between them. The war itself Charles expected to be profitable and he hoped also to end up in control of the Rhine estuary, which would greatly enhance England's commercial position and hence the King's revenues. Success in his plans would be a triumph

Treaty of Dover 1670

WESTERN EUROPE IN THE TIME OF LOUIS XIV

for the King's personal foreign policy and would restore his prestige after the humiliations at the end of the Second Dutch War. The monarchy could emerge more powerful than it had ever been.

In 1672 Louis invaded Holland, and England entered the war on the French side (Third Dutch War, 1672-4). At the same time Charles, who was urged by his advisers finally to solve the problem of the Dissenters unreconciled to his rule, issued a Declaration of Indulgence, which suspended the laws against both Dissenters and Roman Catholics. The Third Dutch War was, from the English point of view, a gamble on a quick victory. It did not come off. The

Third Dutch War 1672-4

89

fighting at sea proved indecisive and commerce-raiding was unproductive. By early 1673 it was necessary to meet Parliament in order to procure more money, and to meet it without the prestige accruing from victory on which Charles had counted. The most contentious issue in the Parliament was the Declaration of Indulgence. The strongly Anglican Commons were furious with the King for suspending the laws, and refused to vote him supplies until he had withdrawn the Declaration. The King was obliged to give way. The Commons, in order to clinch the matter, then passed the Test Act (1673), compelling all who held State offices to receive the Communion according to the Anglican rites. The result of this was that the Catholic Clifford had to resign from the Cabal, and, more important still, that the Duke of York, who soon afterwards declared himself a Catholic, had to resign his command of the navy.

Test Act 1673

Charles saw that the opposition was too strong for him, and, as he had no mind to go on his travels again, he told Louis that he would proceed no farther with his scheme. But Charles dismissed his Chancellor, Lord Shaftesbury (Ashley-Cooper), who suspected that he had been tricked. Shaftesbury, who became the leader of the opposition in Parliament, was a dangerous man to offend. 'It is only laying down my robe,' said the ex-Chancellor, 'and buckling on my sword.' It was a sharp sword, as Charles was to discover. The King formed a new ministry under the direction of Sir Thomas Osborne, who was made Earl of Danby and Lord Treasurer in 1673. Since Danby was a Cavalier and a staunch Anglican, his appointment quietened the Commons for the time being.

Shaftesbury in Opposition

The following year Parliament insisted on England's withdrawing from the Dutch War, and peace was accordingly made with Holland by the Treaty of Westminster of 1674. The Dutch put up a gallant defence against Louis for another four years. As in the great days of the first William of Orange, they had cut the dykes and flooded the country in order to protect themselves. Another William of Orange had been made head of the state, a man whose life was to be spent in

Treaty of Westminster 1674

William of Orange

one long struggle against the power of Louis XIV. William, who was Charles' nephew (son of his sister Mary), was only twenty-two when in the dark hour of 1672 he was called to the government of his country. But though William and the Dutch eventually brought Louis' famous armies to a standstill, their country never fully recovered from the French attack, aided by their so-called ally, England.

3. Whigs and Tories

In the later 1670s Charles II sought to remain on good terms with Louis XIV in order to get as much money out of him as possible and to reduce his dependence upon Parliament. Louis, for his part, since he could not have England for an ally, wished at any rate to keep it neutral. He feared that the anti-Catholic feeling in that country might at any moment boil over into a demand from Parliament for a French war. So he paid Charles to prorogue Parliament as often as possible.

Charles and Louis XIV

Charles' new minister, Danby, did not approve of this pro-French policy, though he did not venture to oppose the King. Danby was as much against France as any man, and was sometimes able to persuade Charles to take measures against Louis. It was due to him that in 1677 the King's niece, Mary of York, married William III of Orange, Louis XIV's most determined opponent. At the time Mary was second in the line of succession to the throne after her father James. This marriage was destined to change the course of English history, for it paved the way for Dutch William to succeed to the Crown.

Marriage of William and Mary 1677

The last ten years of Charles II's reign form one of the most complicated periods in English political history. It was then that the two great historic parties, the Whigs and Tories, were formed. Danby made it his business to form a Court party (later called Tory) from the Cavaliers, based on devotion to the Crown and to the Church of England. Danby was the first party 'manager' in English history: he understood the art of holding a party together by patronage, that is to say, by the award of minor offices to faithful party men.

Danby 1673-9

Shaftesbury

At the same time a Country party (later called Whig) was formed in opposition to the Court. The founder of this party was Anthony Ashley-Cooper, Earl of Shaftesbury, one of the greatest schemers and one of the greatest fighters in English politics. Even the poet Dryden, who said that Shaftesbury's name would be 'to all succeeding ages curst', admitted that the man was a 'daring pilot in extremity'. Just as Danby was party manager in the House of Commons, Shaftesbury was a great organizer of popular opinion outside the House. He formed the Green Ribbon Club in Chancery Lane, and from there organized a system of propaganda, carried on by writers and speakers all over the country.

Titus Oates

The Popish Plot 1678-80

The party of Shaftesbury was founded partly on the old Roundhead opposition to any extension of the royal power, partly on an appeal to the widespread fear and hatred of Roman Catholics. Slavery and popery, he declared, went hand in hand. A chance was soon offered him of exploiting to the full this old religious prejudice, which went back to the days of the Armada and Gunpowder Plot. In 1678 Titus Oates, a disreputable clergyman and one of the greatest liars in history, pretended to reveal a Jesuit 'plot' to murder the king. The plot was Oates' own invention, but he succeeded in convincing others of its truth, and made a deposition before a London magistrate, Sir Edmund Godfrey. Ten days later Godfrey was found murdered, transfixed by his own sword. The murder was assumed to be the work of the Jesuits, and at once the whole country went mad. The wildest rumours were circulated and believed – the Jesuits were going to set fire to London, kill the King, or betray the country to the French. In the panic which ensued, not only in London but all over England, many innocent men lost their lives. A number of Catholics, innocent both of Godfrey's murder and of the alleged plot, were brought to trial, and the perjurer Oates swore away their lives.

Given the kind of man Oates was, it seems incredible that so many should have believed his fabrications. The explanation lies in the atmosphere of fear and suspicion which had grown up in the previous years, largely thanks to Charles II's double-dealing and dishonest policies. His close relations with Louis XIV led many to suspect a scheme to copy Louis' form of absolute government. Charles' contradictory policies, sometimes siding with the Dutch, sometimes with the French, created intense mistrust of the government. It came out in January 1679 that Danby had been a party to the arrangements over one of Louis' cash payments to Charles. Danby had acted unwillingly, and only on the king's express command, but the Commons would not listen to that excuse. They voted his impeachment, and to save his minister's life Charles dissolved Parliament, which had sat for eighteen years (Jan. 1679). The King pardoned Danby, but the new Parliament proceeded with the impeachment, thus asserting the principle that ministers are responsible to Parliament for their actions and Danby was sent to the Tower for five years. 17th century Englishmen expected that a design to destroy their liberties would be accompanied by plans to subvert their religion. In this context, the government's close relations with a self-proclaimed champion of Catholicism like Louis XIV were suspicious. The Declaration of Indulgence that had been issued at the time of the Third Dutch War aroused fears that it was meant chiefly to benefit Catholics. The open Catholicism of James, the heir to the throne, was still more alarming, especially when James' secretary, accused by Oates, was found to be engaged in treasonable correspondence with Louis' Jesuit confessor.

Impeachment of Danby

Shaftesbury's aim was to rid England of the twin dangers of royal absolutism and Catholicism. To achieve it he concentrated on securing the exclusion of the Duke of York from the succession to the throne, on the ground that he was a Roman Catholic. An Exclusion Bill was brought in, and read before the three Parliaments which Charles summoned and dissolved in the course of the next two years (1679-81). It was during the Exclusion Bill debates that the famous names Whig and Tory were first applied to the rival parties. Both names were terms of abuse. Whig originally meant a rebel

Exclusion Bill 1679-81

Whig and Tory

Scottish Presbyterian; Tory, a rebel Irish Papist. The Whigs came to be so called because Nonconformists and their sympathisers were so prominent in the party. The Tories were above all the party of the established Church. The years 1679-81 were marked by bitter party strife: elections were strongly contested, monster petitions were presented and there were some outbreaks of violence.

Thanks largely to Shaftesbury, one measure of permanent importance was passed by a Parliament otherwise engaged in the fierce debates over Exclusion. The Habeas Corpus Act (1679) ensured (as it still does) that no English subject should be kept in prison without being brought to trial as soon as possible for the crime of which he is accused. This famous Bill would have been rejected in the House of Lords but for the practical joke of a Lord who counted one fat peer as ten men!

Habeas
Corpus Act
1679

While the Exclusion question was being debated, Charles sent his brother out of the country, and upheld James' rights himself. The King's behaviour during this panic-stricken time shows him at his best. He remained cool throughout, and indeed he might almost be called the only public man in England who did not lose his head. Perhaps he realised that he was in a far stronger position than his father had been in 1641. A revolt in Scotland was easily crushed and Ireland was quiet. The rise in revenue because of peace and improved financial administration meant that Charles was not short of money. There was little chance that an Exclusion Bill would pass the House of Lords. Charles' policy was to play for time, in the hope that the Whigs would ruin themselves by their violence. In this calculation he proved to be correct. Shaftesbury's first false move was to propose that the Duke of Monmouth, Charles' eldest illegitimate son, should be recognized as his heir, instead of the Duke of York. This offended many people, who still believed that there was something semi-divine about the person of a King, but could not extend their worship of royalty to a King's illegitimate children. The Whigs then tried to prove – though without success – that Charles had been really married to Monmouth's mother, Lucy Walters. Meanwhile, they persisted in the hounding down of the so-called Popish plotters, exploiting a hysteria that was certain to fade in time. Many men were disgusted when old Lord Strafford, aged 69, was condemned on perjured evidence and executed (December 1680).

Execution of Lord Strafford 1680

At the beginning of 1681 the tide began to turn. The anti-Papist fury became less violent, and people no longer believed everything that Oates said. Men who could remember the Civil War began to ask themselves where the strife between Whig and Tory would end. Charles judged that the time was ripe to get rid of Parliament, and the Whigs with it. He had just received a substantial payment from Louis, so he was not anxious on the score of supplies. He decided to meet Parliament at Oxford, away from the city mobs, which were on the Whig side. So Shaftesbury and his friends were obliged to ride through Oxford streets lined with hostile students, who hooted them as they passed by. As soon as Parliament assembled, Charles dissolved it (1681). He never summoned another and the Exclusion Bill was never passed.

Charles dissolves Parliament 1681

Coolness had won, and Shaftesbury found his popularity beginning to fade away, even in London where he had once seemed so strong. The country looked on calmly while Charles proceeded to strike down his enemies. First, he aimed a blow at that Whig stronghold, the City of London He demanded the surrender of London's charter and then appointed a Tory mayor and officers. He followed this up by taking similar action against sixty-six boroughs (1682). Shaftesbury, afraid of arrest, fled to Holland, where he died in the following year (1683).

London Charter 1682

Death of Shaftesbury 1683

Finally the Whigs played into the king's hands by concocting a desperate plot to murder him and his brother at Rye House (1683) on their way back from Newmarket Races. The plot was betrayed and the leaders executed. Lord Russell, one of the Whig leaders, was implicated and condemned to death. Algernon Sidney, another prominent Whig, was next tried before Judge Jeffreys, who (at 35)

Rye House Plot 1683

had just been made Lord Chief Justice of England, and condemned to death on flimsy evidence. Thus the Whig party, for the time being, was utterly broken.

The Whig defeat meant a victory for the Tories. Charles ended his reign in a strong position, but his triumph was not unconditional. He had to respect the interests of the Anglican Church, which had supported him, and to forego any hopes of introducing toleration of Nonconformists or Catholics. He had to allow Anglican gentry and townsmen to dominate county and town government. Otherwise, Charles enjoyed considerable freedom of action and his brother James entered into an unexpectedly stable inheritance when in 1685 Charles had a sudden and fatal seizure. In his last moments he showed the sense of humour which had never deserted him apologizing to the waiting courtiers for 'being such an unconscionable time dying'. Before the end he received the last rites of the Roman Catholic Church from the hands of Father Huddleston, the old priest who had saved his life after Worcester, thirty-four years before.

Death of Charles II 1685

4. James II

Character of James II

James, Duke of York, who now succeeded to the throne as James II, was a very different man from his brother. He entirely lacked Charles' coolness and humour, and thought that every man who opposed him must necessarily be a rebel. It has been said that James never forgot an enemy, and seldom remembered a friend. Stubborn, revengeful, and entirely tactless, he was destined to lose, in the short space of three years, the throne which his brother had preserved and strengthened by a careful exercise of political craft.

Thanks to Charles' triumph over the Exclusion Bill, there was no opposition when James ascended the throne; the country had never been more quiet. No protests were made when the king heard Mass at Whitehall. Parliament met, and not only voted James the whole of the revenue granted to Charles II, but an extra supply of £400,000.

Then came the news that Monmouth had landed at Lyme Regis (June 1685).

Monmouth was in Holland when he heard that his father, King Charles II, was dead. He decided to come to England and proclaim himself King, in the hope that a large number of his uncle's Protestant subjects would support him. But Monmouth was mistaken; he had no large following in England. He raised a small force in Wiltshire, Dorset, and Somerset, but no one from the ruling classes joined it and it was outnumbered by the royal troops, commanded by Lord Feversham and John Churchill, afterwards the famous Duke of Marlborough. One summer night Monmouth and his men, many of them armed only with swords and scythes, tried to attack the royal camp on Sedgemoor. In the darkness they stumbled up against an impassable ditch, and there they were trapped and shot down. Monmouth fled, and was soon afterwards captured. He was brought to London, but, after begging for his life from James in vain, he was executed at Tyburn. His rebellion had lasted less than a month (June-July 1685).

Monmouth's Rebellion 1685

After the battle of Sedgemoor the rebels were cruelly pursued for several weeks by Colonel Kirke, whose soldiers were ironically called 'Kirke's Lambs'. Then the Lord Chief Justice came down to the West, to hold his infamous 'Bloody Assizes', as they were afterwards called. Jeffreys bullied his wretched prisoners, laughed at their sufferings, and showed mercy to none. The worst case was the execution of an old lady, named Alice Lisle, whose only crime was that she had sheltered some fugitives. Altogether 300 persons were hanged, and 840 transported to the West Indies. On his return to London the cruel judge was welcomed by a grateful sovereign, and made Lord Chancellor.

The Bloody Assizes

The completeness of his victory made James feel secure. He did not disband his army, but kept 15,000 troops in camp on Hounslow Heath, near London. Parliament, which met again that November, was suspicious of the King's intentions regarding his standing army, and refused to vote full supplies until he had given some assurances in the matter of religion. But James, with troops of his own, and the hope of money from France, could now afford, so he thought, to be independent. He prorogued Parliament (November 1685), and it never met again during his reign.

It was James' intention to relieve the Roman Catholics in England, as (in his view) the only true believers, of all the disabilities which had been imposed upon them and to enable them to play a full part in the government of the country. He at first hoped to achieve this with the agreement of the Anglican Tories, dominant as a result of the failure of Exclusion. If the Anglicans had co-operated, then he would not have needed to make any fundamental changes to the laws and the constitution.

Unfortunately for James, the Anglicans did not co-operate. Already in November 1685 Parliament attacked James' employment of Catholic officers in the army. The King was overriding the laws, especially the Test Act, which debarred Roman Catholics from holding official positions. James held that the Crown possessed a 'dispensing power', by right of which the king could dispense with the law in particular cases. In virtue of this power he proceeded to appoint Catholics to important positions in Church and State. His own brothers-in-law, Clarendon and Rochester, were dismissed, Clarendon from the governorship of Ireland, Rochester from the Treasury. Catholics were introduced into the Privy Council. Then the king turned to the universities, where he threatened the Anglican monopoly of higher education. A Catholic was appointed Dean of Christ Church, Oxford. At Cambridge the Vice-Chancellor was deprived of his office for refusing to confer a degree on a Benedictine monk. In 1687 the President of Magdalen, Oxford, died, and the Fellows elected a man of their own choice instead of the King's candidate, who was a Catholic. James visited Oxford in person, and in the end he got his way by turning twenty-five of the Fellows out of the College. Their places were taken by Roman Catholics. The

Attack on
Universities

Anglicans vigorously opposed James. In London Bishop Compton orchestrated the opposition of the clergy, while Anglican magistrates throughout the country refused to acquiesce in Catholic freedom of worship.

Finding the Anglicans unco-operative, the King looked for other allies. In 1687 he issued a Declaration of Indulgence, by which he suspended the laws against both Roman Catholics and Dissenters. By this action he hoped to enlist Dissenters' support for his policy. Halifax, who, like Clarendon and Rochester, had been dismissed from the government, wrote a pamphlet – of which 20,000 copies were sold – called a *Letter to a Dissenter* in which he gave the warning: 'You are therefore to be hugged now, only that you may the better be squeezed at another time.' At first, the warning was unheeded, by many Nonconformists, who thanked the King for his concessions.

First Declaration of Indulgence 1687

By the close of the year 1687 James, by his hasty conduct, had alienated the sympathy of his Anglican subjects, the very people who had supported his claim to the throne in the Exclusion crisis. In these circumstances most leading figures simply hoped that James would soon die, leaving the throne to his elder daughter Mary. Mary was herself a Protestant, and she was the wife of the greatest Protestant leader in Europe – William of Orange. During the year 1687 many of the leading lords in England were in communication with William. He was anxious to safeguard his wife's right to the English throne, which might be in danger if James' policies brought about a revival of republicanism. But by the end of 1687 a different danger loomed: it was announced that James II's Queen was pregnant. Should she be delivered of a son, Mary would no longer be heir to the throne and the Anglicans might have to face the prospect of a line of Catholic Kings stretching into the future.

Growth of opposition to James

5. The Revolution of 1688

Second
Declaration of
Indulgence
May 1688

In May 1688 James reissued his Declaration of Indulgence, and gave orders that it should be read in all churches. This was more than the bishops could stand. Seven of them, led by Sancroft, Archbishop of Canterbury, petitioned to be excused from enforcing the order. James promptly sent them to the Tower, and ordered them to be tried for

Trial of the
Seven Bishops
June 1688

libelling the king. As the bishops entered the Tower the very soldiers on guard knelt to receive their blessing. The trial took place; the jury was at first divided; then came the verdict – Not guilty.

There was tremendous excitement in London; bonfires were lit in the streets when the Seven Bishops were acquitted. This was on the 30th June. On the 1st July the Queen, Mary of Modena, gave birth to a son. These two events decided James' fate. The acquittal of the

Birth of the
Prince of
Wales 1688

Seven Bishops was a great blow to his prestige, but the birth of the prince was the turning point. For it was now clear that James' policy would not die with him; his son would in the normal course of events, continue it. But though James II might possibly be tolerated for the rest of his life, the prospect of a Catholic James III was too much. There was only one thing to be done, and that was to summon the aid of the Prince of Orange.

Invitation to
William

The invitation to William was signed by important Whigs and Tories: Henry Sidney and Admiral Russell, who were Whigs and relations of the Rye House conspirators, Danby and Bishop Compton of London who were Tories, and Lumley an ex-Catholic. These men and two other moderates signed the invitation which was carried over to Holland by Admiral Herbert, disguised as a common sailor. William was given to understand that many important men, besides the actual signatories, would go over to his side, including Lord Churchill, James' best general. William was asked to bring an army over to England to restore English liberties. He had already decided to invade his father-in-law's kingdom and begun his preparations.

William's object in accepting the support of the Seven and launching an invasion was to gain control of England and then to use its resources to tilt the balance of power in Europe against Louis XIV. It had become the chief purpose of the Prince's life to curb the power of the would-be tyrant of all Europe. Louis knew that the Dutch were raising an army and a fleet to invade England, but he was determined to strengthen his position in western Germany while the Emperor was distracted by a Turkish war. Once Louis' armies were committed to Germany, William was able to risk invading England.

In November 1688 William set sail from Holland and, helped by a favourable wind, came down the English Channel and landed at Torbay in Devonshire. His was the largest professional army that had invaded England since Roman times. He had 15,000 troops, of whom about 4,000 were English and Scottish soldiers who had served in Holland; the rest were Dutch, Swedes, and Germans. In the west country, as William advanced, the population was friendly; memories of Sedgemoor were too recent to allow of any loyalty to King James.

Landing of William (November)

William advanced into Wiltshire; James led his army as far as Salisbury. But when Lord Churchill rode off in the night to join William, James appears to have undergone a mental breakdown. Suffering a series of nosebleeds, he decided to retreat, and re-entered his capital. There he learnt that his younger daughter, the Princess Anne, had fled to join the enemy. London was in a ferment; the King's hopes were fast dying. Panicking, he summoned a Council of Peers, and issued orders to treat with William. But already he knew that the game was up. While his ambassadors, Halifax and two others, were conferring with William at Hungerford, James fled from the capital on his way to France (December 1688). He had already sent the Queen and the Prince of Wales out of the country.

Final flight of James (December)

The Council of Peers, whom James had summoned, now assumed the government, under Halifax. They invited William to co-operate with them in calling a free Parliament. Then the unwelcome (to William) news arrived that James had been captured and strip-searched at Faversham in Kent. He was brought back to London, but William arranged that some Dutch troops should carry him off to Rochester, where he was allowed to escape for the second time. On Christmas Eve he took a boat to France. He never landed in England again.

Orders were now issued for the summoning of a Convention to settle the succession to the throne. James' flight to France cut the ground from under the feet of Tories who would have preferred to retain him as King, perhaps with his daughter Mary as regent. Mary could be regarded as Queen by hereditary right, since many believed that James' son was not really his, but had been smuggled into the Queen's room in a warming pan. But Mary refused to accept the crown unless it was jointly offered to William; and William refused to be his wife's gentleman usher. So when the Convention met in January 1689, William and Mary were proclaimed King and Queen as joint sovereigns.

William and Mary

The Glorious Revolution, as it was afterwards called, had thus been accomplished in England without bloodshed, and a new era in English history had begun. The Revolution has often been described as the final victory of Parliament in a century-long struggle with the monarchy. Yet the events of 1688 were a triumph for Tories, not just for Whigs, and William III defeated all attempts to impose serious limitations on the essential powers of the Crown. Even the language of Divine Right did not die, but was to be much used when Anne, Mary's younger sister, came to the throne in 1702. In two ways, however, the Revolution determined the future. First, by accepting King William England committed itself to European war against Louis XIV. The war was to change England more profoundly than the Revolution itself did. Second, to ensure that the Nonconformists did not support James II, who offered them toleration, the Anglicans had been compelled to make their own offer of toleration. Hence, the Revolution marked the end of the long effort to force all Englishmen within the confines of a single Church.

The Glorious Revolution

IV

THE EMPIRE UNDER THE STUARTS

THE great discoveries of the Age of Columbus and Vasco da Gama had been followed, in the sixteenth century, by the foundation of the first two colonial empires of the modern world, those of Spain and Portugal. In the seventeenth century three more European colonial empires were founded, those of France, Holland, and England. The rivalries of these five Powers in America, Africa, and Asia form a great part of the colonial history of the seventeenth century.

The founding of these overseas empires was accompanied by a commercial revolution – by a change of trade routes and a great expansion of commerce. The wealth of Europeans was increased, and their comfort was enhanced by new commodities such as tea and coffee, and (from the New World) the potato, cane-sugar, tobacco, and American mahogany. The explorers, missionaries, and merchants of Europe gradually penetrated all lands, and took with them their manners, languages, and institutions. This process of Europeanizing the world, one of the outstanding features of modern history, continued until the collapse of the European empires after the Second World War.

1. The First American Colonies

The project of planting an English colony on the eastern shores of North America had first been undertaken by Sir Walter Ralegh, but this Elizabethan colony did not prosper. Early in the reign of James I the scheme was revived, and a London company was formed to send out colonists to Virginia. These colonists made the first permanent English settlement in North America, landing in Chesapeake Bay in 1607. The first township was called Jamestown, after the King.

Virginia 1607

These early Virginian settlers were not good colonists, and they would probably all have perished from starvation but for the energy of Captain John Smith. This remarkable man was a soldier who had spent a life of amazing adventure fighting Turks and Moors, and now came to pit his skill against Indian braves, and to inspire the Virginians with something of his own spirit. His efforts in the first two years set the colony on its feet. He organized the food supply and set up fortifications against Indian attacks.

Captain John Smith

A few years later the famous tobacco plantations were begun. The soil was suitable, and the crops flourished so well that it was soon found necessary to import slaves from Africa and criminals from England to work the plantations. Tobacco growing was profitable, and in time an aristocracy of rich planters grew up in Virginia. The planters lived in big houses on wide estates, with negroes and 'mean whites' as their dependents.

Tobacco planters

The Virginia Company in England controlled the fortunes of the colony in its early years, and when the Company was abolished in 1624, the Crown took control. There was also a Governor and Council on the spot. In 1619 Governor Yeardley made an interesting experiment. He called an Assembly, consisting of two men from each of the eleven townships in the colony. The Governor, his Council, and the Assembly roughly corresponded to the government of King, Lords, and Commons in England. This Virginia Assembly was the first of those colonial Parliaments which were afterwards instituted throughout the Empire; its first meeting is therefore an important landmark in colonial history.

Virginia Assembly 1619

The next American colony was of a very different character; it was formed by religious exiles from England. Early in James I's reign a few Puritans, mostly from Lincolnshire, disgusted with their treatment in England, left England and sought a refuge at Leyden in Holland. After ten years' residence there some of them decided to emigrate to North America. They were joined by other Puritans from England, and the Pilgrim Fathers, as these exiles were afterwards

Pilgrim Fathers

THE FOUNDATION OF THE AMERICAN COLONIES
A typical southern plantation in its infancy in Savannah, Georgia, in 1734.

called, left Plymouth in the *Mayflower* in September 1620. The same autumn they landed just north of Cape Cod and founded their first township, which they called Plymouth.

Eight years later a larger and more influential body of Puritans formed a company called the Massachusetts Bay Company (1628), which obtained a charter from Charles I in the following year. Without leaving any representatives in England, the whole body of shareholders crossed the Atlantic in 1630 and formed the colony of Massachusetts. This colony prospered from the first. It received a steady flow of immigrants from England during the eleven years of Charles' personal government and the administration of Laud, and by 1640 it had a population of 20,000. *Massachusetts 1628-30*

But though these Puritans had left home to escape from the religious intolerance of Laud, their own government was no less intolerant than his. The first governor, elected by the colonists, was John Winthrop, a man of considerable ability but narrow views. Political rights in Massachusetts, no less than in England, were made *Religious Tyranny* to depend on conformity with a narrow religious creed. This creed was determined by the small circle of strict Puritans who surrounded the governor. Harsh punishments, like flogging and the cutting off of ears, were inflicted on moral offenders and on persons who ventured to differ from their rulers on minor points of religion. A clergyman called Roger Williams, driven from Massachusetts by this persecution, founded the colony of Rhode Island (1636).

New England

Several other Puritan colonies were also formed to the north and south of Massachusetts; some of these, including the original settlement at Plymouth, were absorbed by Massachusetts. Eventually four separate Puritan colonies emerged – Massachusetts, Rhode Island, Connecticut, and New Hampshire; and the whole group was known as New England.

The Puritan colonies were on the whole very prosperous, and continued to receive emigrants from England. The New Englanders tended to be less aristocratic than the Virginians, though narrow religious opinion prevented the growth of a real democracy. Their severance from England was more marked than that of Virginia, because they regarded themselves as exiles rather than colonists.

Newfound-land

Several attempts were made during the early Stuart period to colonize the island of Newfoundland, which had been claimed for England by Sir Humphrey Gilbert under Elizabeth. James I granted a charter to certain Bristol merchants (1610), who planted a small colony at a place called Cupid's Cove.

Later, Lord Baltimore, a Roman Catholic peer, made another settlement in Newfoundland, but it did not prosper. The early history of Newfoundland is chiefly a record of disputes and fights between the French and English fishermen, both of whom claimed possession of the coasts. It was the famous cod fishery, one of the most profitable in the world, which at that time gave the fog-bound island its only value.

Lord Baltimore was also responsible for the beginning of another American colony. He obtained a charter from Charles I to form a colony on the mainland; it was called Maryland in honour of the queen. He was made the proprietor of the colony, and was given absolute rights over its government. Maryland was founded by his second son, Leonard Calvert, who brought the first batch of colonists into Chesapeake Bay, where the town of St. Mary's was founded (1634). The Baltimores were Catholics, but from the first their colony was marked by religious toleration. Like its neighbour Virginia it engaged in tobacco planting and quickly became prosperous.

Maryland 1634

Two blocks of English territory were thus formed during the first half of the Stuart period – New England in the north and Virginia and Maryland in Chesapeake Bay, the two being separated by the Dutch colony of the New Netherlands in the Hudson valley. The French had also begun the colonization of North America, having settled in Acadie (Nova Scotia) and the St. Lawrence valley. In 1608 Quebec was founded by the great French explorer, Samuel Champlain, who also discovered the lake that bears his name and explored the country round Lakes Huron and Ontario. This was the beginning of the French colony of Canada, or New France.

The French in Canada

Hudson

North of Canada an Englishman, Henry Hudson, opened up the Arctic regions round the great bay that was named after him. Hudson made several voyages, some in English vessels, some in the service of the Dutch. He explored the Arctic regions in the service of the English Russia Company, and sailed as far east as Nova Zembla, north of Russia. Then, in Dutch service, he went to North America and discovered the famous river that bears his name (1609). The Dutch built the town of New Amsterdam (now New York) at the mouth of the Hudson River. The explorer sailed on his last voyage, in an English ship, in the following year. He tried to find the North West Passage to Cathay and the East, and discovered instead Hudson Bay. Here he came to the end of his adventures, for his crew mutinied and set him and his son adrift in a small boat. They were never heard of again. The discovery of Hudson Bay gave English traders an opportunity to engage in the fur trade, in competition with the French Canadians.

Hudson River 1609

Hudson Bay 1610

West Indies The French and English also made settlements in some of the West Indian islands which had not been occupied by the Spaniards. The most important English island was Barbados (1625), where the sugar planters made fabulous fortunes. The English also took possession of St. Kitts and Antigua, and began to settle in the uninhabited Bahama Islands. The West Indies depended for their prosperity on the slave trade, which continued to flourish for many generations. The largest West Indian possession of the British was Jamaica, captured under Cromwell's government in 1655. But the trade of Jamaica did not rival that of the much smaller island of Barbados, which was for long regarded as the 'chief jewel in the British crown'.

2. The East India Company

The first European traders in the Indian Ocean were the Portuguese, who established trading stations in the East Indies, in Ceylon, and on the coasts of India itself. The Portuguese supremacy in the East lasted throughout the sixteenth century. Then, at the beginning of the seventeenth century, the English and Dutch entered on the scene. The English East India Company was formed in 1600; the Dutch Company three years later. The profits from the voyage to the Spice Islands were enormous, and East India merchants soon made large fortunes.

The Dutch, however, drove the Portuguese from their trading
Dutch and English stations in the East Indies, and soon established themselves there so firmly that they regarded the presence of the English in the islands as a trespass on their preserves. They were much better organized
Amboyna massacre 1623 than the English, had a larger capital behind them, and were superior in numbers. Consequently the English, like the Portuguese before them, were driven from the East Indies. The end came when the Dutch seized eighteen English merchants at Amboyna, imprisoned

them, and put them to the torture. Then van Speult, the Dutch governor, had ten of the English prisoners executed in the presence of the natives (1623). James I could obtain no compensation for this atrocity; it was left for Cromwell, thirty years later, to do so at the conclusion of the First Dutch War. This was the end of English enterprise in the East Indies, which were left entirely in Dutch hands.

In India itself, however, British fortunes prospered better. The Mughal Empire was about this time at the height of its power and magnificence. The founder of this great empire was a Mongolian adventurer named Babur, who invaded India in 1526 through the Punjab and overthrew the previous Empire of Delhi. Babur's grandson was Akbar (1556–1605), who ruled over all northern and central India. Akbar's empire was one of the greatest in the world in the sixteenth century. His dynasty was Muslim, but he strove to unite the people over whom he ruled, both Moslem and Hindu. Under his son and grandson, Jahangir and Shah Jahan – contemporaries of James I and Charles I of England – the Mughal Empire reached the zenith of its power. This was also the great period of Indian Muslim architecture; the Mughal emperors, it has been said, designed like giants and finished their work like jewellers. The wonderful palaces and tombs built by these monarchs can only be compared with the work of the Pharaohs of Egypt. It was Shah Jahan who built the Palace at Delhi and also the Pearl Mosque and the Taj Mahal at Agra (1630). The Taj Mahal, one of the most famous monuments in the world, was built to contain the tomb of the Emperor's favourite wife.

Mughal Empire

Akbar

Indian Muslim architecture

The first Englishman to visit the court of the Great Mughal was William Hawkins, a relation of the slave-trader. Hawkins travelled to Agra (1607) and obtained permission from the Emperor Jahangir for Englishmen to trade in his dominions. A trading 'factory' or depot was then set up at Surat, which the Portuguese attempted to molest. But Captain Best, with a few ships, so badly defeated a superior Portuguese squadron off Surat (1612) that the Portuguese retired from the neighbourhood. Not long after this the Portuguese, unable to compete with the Dutch and English, abandoned the struggle. They still retained, however, the city of Goa, on the west coast of India, which was once the centre of their eastern empire.

After the opening of the Surat factory other English stations were planted on various parts of the Indian coasts. A small station at the mouth of the Hooghly river (1633) was the beginning of the English connection with Bengal; while the factory called Fort St. George (1639) afterwards grew into the city of Madras. Such were the small beginnings of the Company which was later destined to dictate terms to the Great Mughal, and to rule India in his name.

Other English factories

Some of the activities of the Dutch during this period have a bearing on later British history. The Dutch took possession of the Cape of Good Hope (1652) and used it as a port of call on the route to the East. But the Cape Colony, under Dutch rule, was never fully developed, nor did it extend far inland. Farther south the Dutch navigators explored the northern and western coasts of Australia. Tasman, their most famous explorer, discovered the island now named after him, and also the southern island of New Zealand (1642), named after a province of Holland. The Dutch did not, however, make much use of these discoveries, and it was left for Captain Cook, in the next century, to reveal the eastern coast of Australia.

The Dutch at the Cape

Australia and New Zealand

3. The Mercantile Empire under Charles II

English commercial hostility to Holland continued for many years after the Amboyna Massacre; it led, as we have seen, to the First Dutch War under the Commonwealth and the Second Dutch War under Charles II. The success of the Dutch in the early seventeenth century showed what a small nation, backed by a strong navy and rich colonies, could achieve. The example of Holland inspired both England and France to follow suit.

After the death of Cardinal Mazarin, Louis XIV became his own *premier ministre*, but he appointed the able Colbert as minister of finance and the colonies. Colbert was the founder of the first French colonial empire. He created the French East India Company and organized the colonies in America. At this time, too, the French mapped out the interior of the American continent. Their great explorer, La Salle, sailed down the Mississippi to its mouth in the Gulf of Mexico (1682). After this a new French colony, Louisiana, was formed round the lower Mississippi. The French now controlled the main river system of North America, and the Great Lakes. Their future in America seemed assured.

The government of Charles II was not far behind that of Louis XIV and Colbert in colonial enterprise. The Commonwealth had made a great beginning by restoring the navy, and Cromwell, with his designs on the Spanish Empire, had aimed to expand an English, Protestant empire. This policy was continued by the statesmen of the Restoration, nearly all of whom were keenly interested in the empire. James, Duke of York, Prince Rupert, Clarendon, and Shaftesbury, all took a hand in the development of the colonies. In Charles II's reign the main lines of commercial and imperial policy – known as the mercantile system – developed. Most statesmen and merchants then believed that the wealth of a country could be greatly increased by encouraging and protecting its manufactures and shipping, and by developing colonies; those who held this creed were later known as 'mercantilists'. A rich nation, it was argued, ought to possess colonies, whose trade should be 'regulated' for the benefit of the mother country. In order to protect the colonies, and attack European rivals, there must be a strong navy. Since first Holland, and later France, were engaged in a similar policy, it was inevitable that the mercantile system should lead to war. The desire to possess more colonies, and for the mother country to grow rich and powerful by their acquisition, outweighed all other considerations. The commerce of the First British Empire continued for a century to be regulated, for the benefit

England and France

Colbert and the French Empire

British Empire and the Restoration

Mercantile system

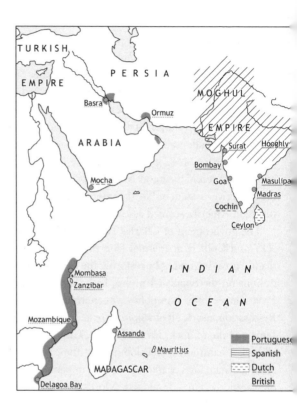

of England, on mercantilist principles – in fact until the loss of the American colonies in George III's reign, after which began the policy of 'free trade' or *laissez-faire* ('letting things alone' instead of 'regulating' them).

Navigation Act 1660

A Navigation Act (1660), passed in the first year of Charles II's reign, laid down the principles on which colonial trade was to be carried on. It re-enacted the provisions of the Commonwealth Navigation Act, i.e. that trade between England and her colonies was to be carried only in English ships. It also ordained that certain

THE COLONIAL AREA: EAST
TIME OF CHARLES II

'enumerated goods', of which the chief were sugar and tobacco, could
be exported from the colonies only to England.

Such was the imperial policy of the Restoration, a policy which
viewed the empire as a means of making England rich, and which
jealously excluded rival nations from sharing in its colonial trade. It
was a policy common to all the European nations which had overseas
possessions. In two important respects, however, the English system
was different from that of its rivals. The colonies were not taxed for
England's benefit, and no attempt was made to interfere in colonial

government. As long as the trade regulations were observed, and they were often evaded by smuggling, the colonies might manage their own taxes and other affairs.

Considerable additions were made to the empire under Charles
Bombay II. He sold Bombay to the East India Company, which thus gained one of its most valuable possessions. The Company's affairs were now so flourishing that its shares sold at a premium of 500 per cent. The attention of the government was also given to West Africa and the West Indies, connected as they were by the lucrative slave trade. A company called the Royal Adventurers (1662), with the Duke of
West Africa York as governor, was formed to regulate the slave raids in West
and West Africa. This company came to grief owing to the persistent attacks
Indies of the Dutch, but it was revived later under the name of the Royal African Company (1672). On the other side of the Atlantic, large fortunes were being made out of sugar in the West Indies; the cheapness of slave labour made these islands valuable out of all proportion to their size. At the end of the century the exports from Barbados alone were worth £300,000 a year, while the exports from all the American mainland colonies combined were worth only £226,000.

Shortly after the Restoration, plans were formed for the development of the land south of Virginia, to be known as Carolina (1663), in honour of the king. This land was granted to eight proprietors, including Clarendon, the Duke of Albemarle (General Monk), and Lord Ashley (Shaftesbury). This association of the leading men in England shows the great interest taken by men close to the government in colonization. The two colonies of North and
Carolina South Carolina were eventually formed by these proprietors, the
1663 colonists being not English emigrants, but settlers from Barbados and Virginia. North Carolina long had an evil reputation on account of the bad character of the settlers. South Carolina owed much of its prosperity to the excellent harbour of the capital, Charleston. Negro slavery was introduced into both colonies.

The year after the granting of the Carolina charter, Charles II authorized his brother, the Duke of York, to take possession of the land between the rivers Connecticut and Delaware. This land was in possession of the Dutch, and the duke's seizure of it was an act of aggression in time of peace. The only excuse that can be given for it is that it followed similar conduct by the Dutch in the East Indies and West Africa. The New Netherlands were neither well populated, nor well defended. Colonel Nicholls, whom the duke sent out to effect the conquest, captured New Amsterdam, the capital, without firing a shot (1664) and the whole colony was easily conquered, the capital being renamed New York in honour of the duke. At the Treaty of Breda (1667), which ended the Second Dutch War, the Dutch recognized the *fait accompli*, and the New Netherlands passed to England. Though these colonies were a useful acquisition, connecting New England with the southern colonies, the real importance of the conquest was not perhaps realized at home at the time. Actually it changed the whole history of North America. The Hudson valley led directly to French Canada, a fact of vast importance later on. The Canadians realized their danger. 'The King of England,' remarked one of them, 'doth grasp at all America.' *(Capture of New York 1664)*

The foundation of the Hudson's Bay Company also dates from Charles II's time. He granted a charter (1670) to the Company, under the governorship of his cousin, Prince Rupert. The Company – the only Tudor or Stuart trading company which lasted into the 20th century – did a flourishing trade in furs. The territories to which it laid claim were of vague dimensions, and later on the traders came in contact with the French Canadians. *(Hudson's Bay Company 1690)*

The last colony to be founded in America in Charles II's reign was Pennsylvania, the only inland colony, but connected with the sea by the Delaware estuary. Its proprietor, William Penn, was a Quaker, the son of that Admiral Penn who had conquered Jamaica. Charles II owed him £16,000, and he made the grant of land in settlement of the debt (1681). Penn began his colony as a refuge for Quakers, but *(Pennsylvania 1681)*

it was open to all Christian sects. His was an enlightened rule, and he insisted on very fair treatment of the Indians. His chief trouble was with his own colonists, who were very quarrelsome. 'For the love of God,' he wrote to them, 'be not so governmentish, so noisy and open in your dissatisfactions.'

Thus twelve out of the Thirteen Colonies[9] of America were

---

[9] The Thirteen Colonies: four in New England – Massachusetts, Rhode Island, New Hampshire, and Connecticut; three formed out of the Dutch colonies – New York, New Jersey, and Delaware; Pennsylvania; Virginia and Maryland; and the two Carolinas. The thirteenth colony, Georgia, was planted in the next century – 1733.

THE COLONIAL AREA: WEST
TIME OF CHARLES II

founded in the reigns of the Stuart Kings, and during the same period the foundations of the future British dominion in India were laid. The Stuart Kings had little to do with these developments, beyond furnishing charters to trading companies and groups of men organizing colonies and imposing trade regulations. The English state was too weak and the colonies too far away for any policy other than benign neglect to be feasible. Altogether perhaps a third of a million people left English shores to settle in the Americas in the course of the 17th century.

It is interesting to note the relative importance of the various Stuart colonies at the time and later. The West Indies, then valued most highly, became in the 19th century a comparatively unimportant part of the Empire; from the few small factories in the East the Indian Empire developed; while the North American colonies became part of the United States of America. South Africa, Australia, and New Zealand were then undeveloped countries, all nominally Dutch possessions, while Canada was in the hands of the French.

V

THE CONQUEST OF IRELAND

1. The Tudors

THE two islands of Great Britain and Ireland lie so near together that they inevitably have a close relationship. Nevertheless, for the greater part of her history, Ireland has taken her separate way and resisted, often successfully, the dominance of her larger neighbour. The Romans never entered Ireland, though it was a Roman citizen, St. Patrick, who introduced Christianity in the fifth century, and inaugurated what is known as the Golden Age of Irish learning and literature.

Ireland and England

The first attempt to conquer Ireland from Britain was made in 1170 when Strongbow, a baron from South Wales, sailed across St. George's Channel from Pembroke. Henry II then took the title of Lord of Ireland, a title which was borne by his descendants. Direct English rule did not extend beyond the Pale – a strip of land along the east coast from Dundalk to Dublin, seldom more than thirty miles wide. Beyond the Pale, the King exercised authority through his ties with the great lords of the Gaelic areas; they in turn controlled the lesser landowners. Many of these great lords were descendants of the original Norman conquerors. In the later Middle Ages Ireland suffered from its position on the periphery of Europe. It remained poor and it was many centuries since its monastic culture had made a vital contribution to the Christianization of the west.

Irish anarchy

The English conquest of Ireland was first seriously undertaken in Tudor and Stuart times. Sir Edward Poynings was sent over to Ireland by Henry VII to assert the supremacy of the English Parliament; but government was largely delegated to trusted nobles, especially to the Earls of Kildare. For a long time, they were able to satisfy the interests of the English Kings while managing Gaelic lords in accordance with their own customs. This system broke down in the 1530s, when Henry VIII needed to tighten his control in order to make sure that Charles V did not try to use Ireland against him. After the revolt, surrender and execution of the 10th Earl of Kildare, Henry adopted a policy of direct rule and took the title of King of Ireland. He dispatched an army to enforce obedience, while setting about the task of anglicizing Ireland by promoting the use of English law, dress and language.

Ireland under Henry VIII

It was in Elizabeth's reign that Anglo-Irish relations took a more sinister turn: the conquest of Ireland showed the English at their worst. In the first place, Englishmen regarded the Irish as savages, and made no pretence of considering Irish wishes or feelings. Secondly, religious differences now widened the breach between the two peoples. The English government insisted on introducing the English Prayer Book into Irish churches, but till late in Elizabeth's reign, no attempt was made to educate a Protestant governing class. Instead, many Irishmen were educated abroad in Catholic Europe, so that the island received a steady supply of Catholic priests. By the end of the century, they were aided by a Jesuit mission. As Elizabeth pursued the policy of planting English colonies in Ireland, it was not surprising that Irish Catholicism and Irish patriotism became allied. Elizabeth's Catholic enemies, the Pope and the King of Spain, were not slow to take advantage of Irish resentment against England. Philip of Spain sent two military expeditions to assist in rebellions against Elizabeth. All this accounts for, though it does not excuse, the ferocity of the English rule. The English garrisons were surrounded by a hostile population, who hated them as foreigners and heretics. On the other hand, the Irish were eager to help Jesuits and Spaniards to use their country as a base from which to attack England.

Elizabethan conquests – its ferocity

Ireland was, in consequence, seething with rebellion throughout Elizabeth's reign. The two most serious risings were in Munster and Ulster. In Munster (1579-83) the rising was organized by the Earl

IRELAND AT THE TURN OF THE SEVENTEENTH CENTURY

of Desmond, and assisted by a Spanish force of 600 men which landed at Smerwick (Kerry). The English put down the rebellion, captured and massacred the Spaniards, and hunted the Irish rebels like animals. By the time this war of extermination was over, Munster was practically a desert. A plan was then adopted that had been tried in Mary's reign, when two counties – called King's County and Queen's County after Philip and Mary – were planted with English colonists. Large districts of Munster were treated in similar fashion; the native owners of the soil were expelled and English colonists took their places. Among these colonists were Sir Walter Ralegh, who introduced potato-growing on his estate at Youghal, and Edmund Spenser the poet, who wrote the *Faerie Queene*, his most famous poem, at Kilcolman House (Cork).

Desmond's Rebellion 1579-83

Plantations in Munster

A more serious rebellion took place in Ulster, and raged during the last eight years of the Queen's reign (1595-1603). It was led by Tyrone's Rebellion 1595-1603 Hugh O'Neill, Earl of Tyrone, and Hugh Roe, the head of the O'Donnells. Tyrone inflicted a severe defeat on an English army at the Yellow Ford on the River Blackwater near Armagh in 1598. The rebellion then began to spread, and there were risings all over Ireland, even in Leinster the most anglicized province. Tyrone seemed on the verge of establishing an independent and united Catholic Ireland. Reluctantly, Elizabeth was compelled to commit herself to the expensive project of the conquest of the island. She sent her favourite, Essex, with a large army to Ireland (1599), but Essex did nothing except make a truce with Tyrone. He was replaced (1600), as viceroy, by Lord Mountjoy, a man of great ability. Soon afterwards the King of Spain sent an army of 5,000 men (1601), who landed at Kinsale (Cork). Tyrone marched into Munster to join them, but Mountjoy beat him, and also brought about the surrender of the Spanish force, thus breaking the back of the rebellion. The viceroy then turned on the Irish, and began the systematic starvation of the countryside. Tyrone submitted just after Elizabeth died. Ireland, conquered but sorely embittered, lay at the feet of the viceroy.

2. The Stuarts

The Queen's successor, James I, continued the policy of plantations which had already been tried in Munster after the suppression of the Plantation of Ulster 1608-11 Desmond rebellion. James' plantation of Ulster was the largest ever carried out in Ireland: nearly the whole province was made into an Anglo-Scottish colony (1608-11). Tyrone and his fellow leaders had fled the country, and this was made the excuse for a wholesale confiscation of land. The City of London was granted the town of Derry, which was colonized by Londoners and renamed Londonderry. The plantation of Ulster had far-reaching effects. It changed the whole character of the northern province, and caused that cleavage between northern and southern Ireland which remains to the present day. The Ulster colonists, besides being of different race, were of different religion; they were mostly English Puritans and Scottish Calvinists. Thus the foundations of Protestant Northern Ireland (1611) and, within a few years, of the British colonies in America (1607-20), were laid in the reign of James I.

Charles I's deputy in Ireland (1633-40) was Thomas Wentworth, who described his Irish policy in the famous word 'Thorough'. Wentworth kept Ireland in order by means of a well-disciplined army such as his master never had in England. He also doubled the revenue, put down piracy in the Irish Sea, and encouraged native industries, including that of Irish linen. But he was ruthless to anyone who opposed him, and earned himself the name of Black Tom Tyrant. Just as he was preparing a fresh expulsion of native landowners – in Connaught – he was recalled to help Charles to deal with the dangerous situation which had arisen in Britain.

Wentworth in Ireland 1633-40

The withdrawal of the strong hand of Strafford, coupled with the king's difficulties in England, had an inevitable reaction in Ireland. A formidable rebellion broke out in the autumn of 1641, when the conquered people rose in a frantic effort to redress the wrongs they had suffered since Elizabeth's time. The ferocity of Mountjoy's conquest, the injustices of the Munster and Ulster plantations, the persecution of the Catholic religion – all these were bitter memories, which were now to be ruthlessly avenged. The Ulster Protestants were driven from their houses and lands; perhaps three thousand persons were killed outright, and many more died of hunger.

Rebellion of 1641

Neither King nor Parliament could at this moment spare troops to conquer Ireland, and the country relapsed into anarchy. When Charles I was dead, so great was the general hatred of Puritans and the fear of a Puritan rule in Ireland that, for a brief period, all parties united under the Earl of Ormonde to support Charles II. It was then that the Commonwealth government sent over Oliver Cromwell to write another page of Irish history in letters of blood.

Cromwell in Ireland 1649-50

IV A HISTORY OF BRITAIN 1603-1714

Drogheda
1649

Ireton

Cromwell landed in 1649. He took Drogheda and Wexford, where fearful massacres took place. Writing after the slaughter at Drogheda, Cromwell said: 'I forbade them to spare any that were in arms in the town; and I think that night they put to the sword about 2000 men ... When they submitted their officers were knocked on the head, and every tenth man of the soldiers killed; and the rest shipped for the Barbadoes ... I am persuaded this is a righteous judgment of God upon these barbarous wretches, who have imbrued their hands in so much innocent blood.' He left General Ireton to continue these methods and complete the conquest. The whole country was starving, and its last defenders died in waste and silent places. No less ruthless than the Elizabethans, the Puritans showed no mercy to the conquered. When Cromwell became Protector, Ireton's work was done. One-third of the population of Ireland had perished in war or from famine.

The
Cromwellian
landlords

Cromwell actually contemplated driving the whole native population beyond the Shannon. Around two-thirds of the land of Ireland changed hands, as estates were given to former soldiers who had fought in Ireland and also to speculators who had invested in Parliament's war effort in return for the promise of Irish lands. But the Cromwellian landlords married Irish wives, and their children in time forgot their English religion and ancestry. Ireland remained Irish; it also remained Catholic. But the 'curse of Cromwell' added one more bitter memory to the list of Irish wrongs.

Under the Restoration Ireland was happier. Charles II was not a religious persecutor, and there was far less persecution in Ireland than in England under the Clarendon Code. There would have been less still, had not any relaxation of the anti-Catholic laws in Ireland provoked alarm and protest in England. The government evicted some, though by no means all, of the Cromwellian landlords:[10] land

---

[10] Before 1641 the Protestants owned about one-third of the cultivable land of Ireland; after Cromwell's conquest over nine-tenths; after 1685 about two-thirds.

remained a cause of deep bitterness among dispossessed Catholics. But free trade, which Cromwell had established throughout the British Isles, was done away with at the Restoration, and Ireland, like Scotland, was treated as a foreign country in matters of trade. The export of Irish cattle to England was prohibited (1666), and the Irish were also forbidden, under the Navigation Act, to trade with the American colonies. Nonetheless, by the 1670s Ireland began to prosper, as was evident from the growth of Dublin, which may have tripled in size during Charles II's reign. Despite fears of Irish Catholic plots at the time of the Popish Plot in England, Ireland was the most stable of Charles' three kingdoms.

Under James II, the foundation upon which all the monarchs since Elizabeth had based their Irish policy was challenged. In 1687 James appointed a Catholic lord deputy, Tyrconnel, who proceeded to threaten the Protestant ascendancy in the country. Protestants lost control of the town corporations and it was feared that the Protestant land settlement might not survive. The effect was to build up for James II a strong following in Ireland, just as he was losing his bases of support in England. Unfortunately for the Catholic Irish, this meant that when William III took over in England, he would not feel secure until he had destroyed James' Irish following in yet another war of conquest, the third in a century.

DATE SUMMARY: STUART PERIOD II (1642-88)

BRITISH ISLES   ABROAD

THE CIVIL WAR (1642-9)

BRITISH ISLES	ABROAD
1642-6 First Civil War	1642 Richelieu died
1643 Solemn League and Covenant	1643 Louis XIV accession
1644 Battle of Marston Moor	Mazarin chief minister
1645 Battle of Naseby	
1648 Second Civil War. Battle of Preston	
1649 Charles I executed	

THE REPUBLIC (1649-60)

BRITISH ISLES	ABROAD
1649-53 Commonwealth	
1649 Cromwell in Ireland	
1650 Battle of Dunbar	
1651 Battle of Worcester	1652-4 First Dutch War
1653-8 CROMWELL PROTECTOR	1655 Spanish War. Capture of Jamaica
1657 Humble Petition and Advice	
1658 Cromwell died	
1658 Battle of Dunkirk	
1659 End of the Protectorate	1658-1705 Leopold I Emperor

CHARLES II (1660-85)

BRITISH ISLES	ABROAD
1660 Restoration	1660 Portuguese Alliance
1661-79 Cavalier Parliament	1661-1715 Louis XIV's personal rule
1662 Act of Uniformity	1663 Carolina
1665-6 Plague and Fire	1664-7 Second Dutch War
	1664 New York taken
1666-1710 Wren's rebuilding	1665-1700 Charles II King of Spain
1667 Fall of Clarendon	
Milton's *Paradise Lost*	
1670 Secret Treaty of Dover	1670 Hudson's Bay Company.
	1672-1702 William III of Orange,
	Stadtholder, Holland.
1673 Test Act	1672-4 Third Dutch War
1678-80 Popish Plot	
1679-81 Exclusion Bill	
1679 Habeas Corpus Act	1681 Pennsylvania
1683 Rye House Plot	1683 Defeat of Turks at Vienna

JAMES II (1685-8)

BRITISH ISLES	ABROAD
1685 Monmouth's Rebellion	1685 Revocation of Edict of Nantes
1687 Newton's *Principia*	
Declaration of Indulgence	
1688 Trial of 7 Bishops	1688 Louis XIV attacked Germany
Birth of James, Old Pretender	

1688 THE REVOLUTION

VI

The Age of Newton and Wren

1. Literature: Puritan and Cavalier

WHEN Charles 11 was restored to the throne John Milton,[11] who had been one of Cromwell's secretaries, was a comparatively old man, bearing the afflictions of poverty and blindness with patience and courage. In 1667 he finished *Paradise Lost*, one of the greatest poems in the English language. The epic tells of the fall of Lucifer from heaven to hell, of his visit to earth, and of the destruction which he wrought in the Paradise which God had made there for the parents of mankind. It is written in blank verse of a quality which has caused Milton to be described as the last of the Elizabethans. Poor and old as he became, and disappointed in his life's work, he yet retained a sense of beauty which made him capable upon occasion of descriptions of unforgettable loveliness, and of the noble pathos of such lines as these, in which he refers to his blindness:

Milton
1608-74

> Thus with the year
> Seasons return; but not to me returns
> Day, or the sweet approach of even or morn,
> Or sight of vernal bloom, or summer's rose,
> Or flocks, or herds, or human face divine;
> But cloud instead, and ever-during dark
> Surrounds me, from the cheerful ways of men
> Cut off, and, for the book of knowledge fair,

---

[11] In his pamphlets Milton had powerfully expressed the opinions of the Puritan party. In his *Areopagitica* (1644), the most famous of his prose writings, he laid down for all time the principles on which the freedom of the press is based.

Presented with an universal blank
Of Nature's works, to me expunged and rased,
And wisdom at one entrance quite shut out.

(Paradise Lost, iii.)

Milton had allied himself with a party which earned a reputation for a bigoted hatred of gaiety and beauty. Some of his friends were undoubtedly of this narrow and intolerant cast of mind; but a consideration, to name only two men, of the work of Milton and his fellow secretary and poet, Andrew Marvell, is in itself enough to dispose of the mistaken idea that Puritanism is merely another name for an unreasoning hatred of what is gracious and beautiful. The Puritans were serious-minded men who detested the looseness which, in their opinion, was undermining their country's life and religion. Hence their hatred of everything which was associated in their minds with courts, palaces, and those

luxurious cities, where the noise
Of riot ascends above their loftiest towers,
And injury and outrage; and, when night
Darkens the streets, then wander forth the sons
Of Belial, flown with insolence and wine.

(Paradise Lost, i.)

Bunyan
1628-88

The second great epic of Puritanism, *The Pilgrim's Progress,* was the work of a brazier of small education, John Bunyan. He was a convert to Puritanism in its most extreme form, and was much distressed by what he considered the wickedness of his early life. In 1653 he joined a Puritan sect recently formed in Bedford. In the first year of the Restoration he was committed to gaol (under the Conventicle Act of 1593) for preaching in a farm-house. 'He hath (so ran the charge) devilishly and perniciously abstained from coming to church to hear divine service, and is a common upholder of several unlawful meetings and conventicles, to the great disturbance and distraction of the good subjects of this kingdom, contrary to the laws of our sovereign lord the king.' Bunyan was imprisoned for twelve years (1660-72); and it was during this time that he began the book that has made his name immortal. Though so differently placed in life, Bunyan resembles Milton in his religious outlook; his work is based upon the English Bible. There is hardly a line in *The Pilgrim's Progress* but reminds the reader how deeply he had drawn upon that well of noble and simple English. Consider the opening, so simple and direct and vivid:

His imprisonment 1660-72

The Pilgrim's Progress

> As I walked through the wilderness of the world, I lighted on a certain place where there was a Den, and I laid me down in that place to sleep; and, as I slept, I dreamed a dream. I dreamed, and behold, I saw a man clothed with rags, standing in a certain place, with his face from his own house, a book in his hand, and a great burden upon his back. I looked, and saw him open the book, and read therein; and as he read he wept and trembled; and, not being able longer to contain, he brake out with a lamentable cry, saying, 'What shall I do?'

Many of the ideas of Milton and Bunyan, particularly their grim preoccupation with death and damnation, may be not much to the taste of the modern reader; yet their work continues to be read – *Paradise Lost* because it is one of the world's most noble and scholarly poems, *The Pilgrim's Progress* because it is an intensely human story, told with a dramatic vividness and a sense of character and a burning sincerity which stamp it as a great work of art.

There are few greater contrasts in English history than that between the age of the Puritan Republic and the age of Charles II. The Restoration meant far more than the overthrow of republican government and the return of monarchy: it meant the end of a great experiment in religious and social life. Since the Puritans first

Charles at the Restoration

appeared in the reign of Elizabeth, nearly a century before, earnestness in religion had been the dominant note in English life. With the Restoration all this was changed, and the difference was seen in the gaiety of Court and town and the revival of the theatre. But the change went deeper than this: it was reflected in many departments of life, in the Church, in literature, and in the new interest in science.

The Clergy
The bishops and clergy of the Church of England were, during the century following the Restoration, an orthodox and distinguished body of men; but they disliked religious enthusiasm, which savoured too much of the sects which they had overthrown, and they saved their enthusiasm for politics. The great majority of the clergy were Royalists, and preached the duty of submission to the Lord's Anointed. They bitterly hated the Church of Rome and all its works, a passion which they shared with the majority of Englishmen.

Restoration Literature
Religious indifference was especially prevalent among the courtiers of Charles II, and it was plainly reflected in literature. The most characteristic writing of the Restoration appears in its satires, its comedies, and its essays. The writers of the day, taking their cue from the King, paid very little attention to the great Elizabethan literature, and very much (though often not so much as they pretended) to French ideas, methods, and styles. They avoided seriousness, and produced no tragedies which can be compared with those of Shakespeare, whose fame greatly declined, not to revive until the eighteenth century. Wit and polish were the two qualities by which the writers of the day set most store, and for which Restoration Comedy is particularly renowned. Its most esteemed writers were Congreve (*The Way of the World*), Wycherley (*The Country Wife*), and Farquhar (*The Beaux' Stratagem*), and the plays named are still performed.

Dryden 1631-1700
Dryden, the leading literary man of the time, wrote much for the theatre, and in a great variety of styles. In satire Dryden was most at his ease and most successful. In the masterly use of wit, irony, and

sarcasm he is equalled only by Alexander Pope in the next century. Satire
His *Absalom and Achitophel*, which deals with the politics of the time,
is a masterpiece, while in lighter vein his *MacFlecknoe* is exceedingly
amusing to read. Some of Dryden's odes, particularly the bold and
stirring *Alexander's Feast*, are still famous.

Another satirist of genius was Samuel Butler, author of *Hudibras*, Butler's
the name he gave to Sir Samuel Luke, the Puritan knight under *Hudibras*
whom Bunyan served in the Civil War. Butler's caricature of the
Presbyterians might apply to any of the Puritan sects, as seen through
the eyes of the Restoration:

A sect whose chief devotion lies
In odd, perverse antipathies,
In falling out with that or this
And finding somewhat still amiss;
More peevish, cross, and splenetic
Than dog distract or monkey sick;
That with more care keeps holyday
The wrong than others the right way;
Compound for sins they are inclined to
By damning those they have no mind to:
Still so perverse and opposite,
As if they worshipped God for spite.

2. The Rise of Modern Science

The greatest men of the seventeenth or Stuart century were not
hostile to religion; indeed, like Boyle or Wren, they were often
orthodox believers. Nevertheless, the scientific spirit, destined to be
so important to the future of the world, took hold of many minds in
this century, while belief in magic and religious fanaticism declined.

Modern science dates from the discoveries of the Renaissance. Although in the sixteenth century attempts were made to investigate the principles of several sciences, little of permanent value was achieved, apart from the researches of the astronomer Kepler (1571-1630) into the laws governing the motion of the planets. Kepler's work laid the foundation of modern astronomical science. The introduction of the use of logarithms (1614) by Napier greatly lightened the labour of astronomical calculations, while the invention of the micrometer (1639) by Gascoigne converted Galileo's telescope into an instrument of precision, adapted for exact measurement.

Astronomy

Pure mathematics had progressed hardly at all beyond the stage to which the early philosophers had brought it. The study of geometry followed the lines laid down by the ancient Greeks, and that of algebra those of the Arab teachers. A notable step forward was taken when two Frenchmen, Descartes (1596-1650) and Pascal (1623-62), began to apply algebraical methods to the solution of geometrical problems. An even more important advance was made when Newton (1642-1727) and Leibniz (1646-1716) worked out the Infinitesimal Calculus, which has proved of the utmost service to workers in every branch of science and has contributed materially to the development of modem engineering. Newton's work was not confined to mathematics, but embraced also achievements of outstanding importance in mechanics and astronomy.

Mathematics

Sir Isaac Newton was born near Grantham, and entered Trinity College, Cambridge, in the year of the Restoration. At the early age of twenty-three he was made Professor of Mathematics, which appointment he held for twenty-five years. His researches led him to enunciate certain fundamental principles of mechanics, known as the laws of motion and the law of gravitation. He was able to show by mathematical proofs that these laws could account for all motion on earth and the observed movements of the heavenly bodies. These and other scientific doctrines he set forth in his *Principia Mathematica*, published in 1687. Notwithstanding his immense contribution to the

Newton

SIR ISAAC NEWTON (1642-1727)
Engraving from a picture by J. A. Houston

sum of human knowledge, Newton was notably modest, and compared his discoveries to those of a child who has gathered a few shells on the shore of a boundless ocean; if he had seen farther than some men, it was because he stood 'on the shoulders of giants' – a graceful compliment to his predecessors. Prompted by Newton's astronomical researches, his friend and pupil, Halley (1656 –1742),

Halley

investigated the motion of comets, and discovered (1682) the periodicity of the famous comet that bears his name.

In the realm of physics, too, some degree of advance has to be recorded. The principle of the barometer was discovered by an Italian experimenter named Torricelli (1608-47), and this in turn led to the discovery by Robert Boyle (1627-91) of the relation between the volume and pressure of gases, known as Boyle's law. Boyle became known as the father of modern chemistry. He published in 1667 a work called *The Sceptical Chymist* in which he boldly challenged the theories held at that time regarding the constitution of matter, and put forward the view that all matter is composed of minute particles – the basis of the atomic theory of later days. Boyle was one of a small group of men, including Newton and Ray, who founded during the Civil War a society called the Invisible College, which preceded the Royal Society. The Society itself was founded under royal patronage in 1662. Its main work was to be the transmission and verification of investigations reported by individual scientists. Its foundation shows that already scientific activity was prestigious and thought important.

Boyle

Two Englishmen, Ray and Woodward, devoted much time to the systematic classification of animals, plants, and rocks, the result of their work being published in 1695. In the realm of human anatomy progress was marked by the discovery of the circulation of the blood by Harvey (1578-1657). Later the microscope enabled observers to enlarge the field of Harvey's researches by studying the composition of the blood. These men, and others like them, extended the limits of man's knowledge of the material universe, and laid the foundations of the vast amount of scientific information which grows with each successive generation of workers, and which serves to give men ever-increasing command over the forces of nature.

Ray and
Woodward

Harvey

3. English Life under Charles II

Perhaps to us the most astonishing fact about Stuart England is that there were only 5 or 5.5 million people in it. In Charles II's day much of the north of England was sparsely populated, though the Yorkshire dales were fully cultivated and throve on the woollen industry. But all over England in the Stuart century agriculture had been changing and production increasing, as the fenlands were drained, the forests cut down and superior farming techniques adopted. The conventional idea of unchanging villages, nestling round their medieval churches, contains only partial truth.

Population of England

Villages changed partly because they were not isolated from the rest of the country. The growth of towns had large effects on village economies. Hardly anywhere in southern England escaped the influence of London, which contained a tenth of the population of the whole country and had an insatiable appetite for wheat, malt, meat, cheese and other foodstuffs. London also needed coal from the collieries of Northumberland and Durham, whose miners' needs stimulated agriculture in the north-east. England was not bound together simply by economic ties. An educational revolution in the century after 1570 or so had done much to create unifying cultural bonds. An enormous effort was made to furnish the parishes with resident graduate clergy who could do what Protestant clergy were supposed to do, that is to preach regularly. In the proliferating grammar schools the gentry received a largely standardized education in the ancient classics and the Protestant religion and many then proceeded to spend time at Oxford or Cambridge and one of the Inns of Court, where numbers of students rose dramatically under Elizabeth and the early Stuarts. Yet the educational expansion of this period did not touch all classes of society. Education reflected status and wealth, and if literacy had become universal among the gentry and professional classes and common among prosperous farmers, it was still rare among agricultural labourers.

The county clergy

In Stuart times, Englishmen ceased to starve. In Cumbria in the 1620s there was a local food shortage so severe that some people died of starvation, but thereafter population grew less rapidly than food supplies, while improved communications ended the era of localized famines. But there was still a problem of chronic underemployment, since many who needed work all the time could find it for only part of the year. The maintenance of these people was a perpetual problem. The Elizabethan Poor Law was the instrument which dealt, or attempted to deal, with this problem; it was amended by an important Act passed in 1662. The Poor Law administrators in London were too often burdened by vagrants who wandered into the capital in search of employment, and became a charge on the rates. Parliament passed an Act (1662) empowering local authorities to remove such persons back to their place of birth, where alone they could claim relief. This forcible removal of a man from one parish where he chose to reside to another was an extremely harsh proceeding. The Act caused much suffering, for it prevented the mobility of labour and chained the unemployed to their native places where often there was no work to be had.

Legal settlement 1662

It was no gentle England over which Charles II reigned. Fighting in various forms, and rough sports, were the delight of all classes. The cruel sports of cock-fighting and bear-baiting were very popular. It is possible that men were less brutal than their grandfathers in Tudor times, but they were brutal enough. In London it was considered one of the sights of the town to watch the wretched lunatics at Bedlam; and men arranged parties to gaze at the whipping of the women prisoners at Bridewell. All the prisons were, as Macaulay says, hells on earth, where the victims of the law lived in conditions of unspeakable foulness, and contracted the most loathsome diseases.

Sports

English people in the seventeenth century were quarrelsome to a degree that now seems incredible. Fighting in the streets was a common occurrence; men were continually fighting duels, while even Oxford dons were known to give each other black eyes. A French

Fighting

ambassador made this comment on the English character: 'When I reflect that this land produces neither wolves nor venomous beasts, I am not surprised. The inhabitants are far more wicked and dangerous.' Drunkenness was a national vice, and few were free from it. Puritan moral severity can be explained partly by the nature of the country in which they lived – an England which was 'merry' indeed, for men were often drunk; a fighting, brawling, rowdy England; an England where the people were sometimes wilder than the beasts. *Drunkenness*

The towns of Stuart England were none of them large, except London, which contained half a million people. The next largest towns were Bristol and Norwich, with 30,000 each. The county towns all had a local importance greater than they have today. York, Shrewsbury, Exeter, and Norwich ranked as provincial capitals for the north, west, south-west, and East Anglia respectively; and the difficulty of getting to London added to their importance. But, by our standards, all the towns were small. Samuel Pepys, visiting Bristol in 1668, remarked with astonishment on the fact that he could look round him and see nothing but houses. *Towns* *Provincial capitals*

The roads which connected the towns were unbelievably bad. In winter they were almost impassable for any kind of vehicle, and coaches which attempted a journey were apt to get stuck fast in the mud. Besides the discomfort of cold and fatigue which this slow progress involved, there was the danger of attack from highwaymen, who infested all the roads. The fastest method of travel was on horseback; the mails were carried strapped to the saddle on pack-horses. The condition of the roads tended to worsen as the traffic using them increased with the growth of population and internal trade. For this reason, some improvements were made on the main roads in Charles II's reign. It was then possible in a stagecoach to do the journey from Oxford to London (55 miles) in twelve hours. From London to York took four days in summer, six in winter; such was the speed of the wonderful 'flying coaches'. The coaching inns of England were excellent; food, drink, and entertainment were all *Roads and Transport* *Inns* plentiful, and, after such journeys, we may agree that the travellers needed them. The shortcomings of the roads meant that the 700 miles of navigable river were utilized for moving bulk goods like coal, corn and salt. A multitude of small projects were undertaken by private individuals to dredge river beds and circumvent weirs. Inland ports like Bedford and Wisbech began to flourish and the economic integration of England was considerably advanced.

London   London contained a tenth of the population of England; it was seventeen times larger than the second biggest town, Bristol. Before the Fire the houses were mostly made of wood, and the streets were little better than alleys. Down the centre of each ran a river of filth,

Lack of   for London was then innocent of sanitation. The Thames itself, though
sanitation   it was London's chief means of communication and always covered with barges conveying passengers, was foul with sewage. There was a large annual death roll, particularly among children; there was a surplus of deaths over births in the city, whose population was maintained and increased by immigration from the countryside. The stench of the city, particularly in summer-time, was well nigh intolerable.

Extent of   Old London, with its walls still standing, thirty feet high in some
London   places, did not extend far west of the Strand. The Oxford Road – the modern Oxford Street, the busiest street in London – still ran between hedges. There was no Embankment, and people descended to the river by crazy steps built down the mud banks. Merchants lived and slept in the City, instead of deserting it at night for a more distant abode. The houses of the wealthy were not placed apart, in suburbs, but built haphazard, often with a stinking alley on one side and an alehouse on the other. Rowdy mobs sometimes hooted my lady's coach as she passed along the narrow, cobbled streets, lit at night by a footman carrying a torch before her.

              England was very seldom free from plague at any time before the
Plague of   eighteenth century; nor, in the absence of sanitation, can we wonder
London   at this. A plague at the accession of James I had carried off 30,000
1665   people. The Great Plague of London, in 1665, was one of the worst

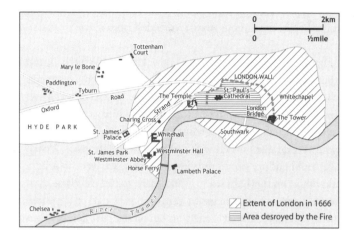

CENTRAL LONDON, SHOWING THE SIZE OF THE CITY IN 1666

of its kind. A hundred thousand Londoners died in six months; it was a time of horror, when all men fled from the once crowded streets. 'What a sad time it is,' said Pepys, 'to see no boats upon the river; and grass grows all up and down Whitehall court, and nobody but poor wretches in the streets!'

After the Plague came the Great Fire, which raged for five days (2-7 September 1666) and burnt up half London. The area destroyed was the heart of the City, from the Tower to Fleet Street. London was expanding both eastwards and westwards in Charles II's time; the untouched parts were therefore Westminster and the modern West End, and the slums of Whitechapel and Stepney to the east of the Tower. It was unfortunate that these slums were not destroyed, for the terrible housing conditions there remained unaltered for centuries. Old St. Paul's, together with eighty-eight other churches, was destroyed. The City had to be rebuilt, brick and stone taking the place of the old walls of lath and plaster.

Great Fire
September
1665

The sight of the Fire was one which those who saw it never forgot. Samuel Pepys, the famous diarist, thus describes it:

Pepys and the Fire

'Having seen as much as I could now, I away to Whitehall, and there walked to St. James' Park … and walked to my boat; and there upon the water again, and to the fire up and down, it still increasing, and the wind great. So near the Fire as we could for smoke; and all over the Thames, with one's face in the wind, you were almost burned with a shower of fire drops … When we could endure no more upon the water, we went to a little ale-house on the Bankside … and there stayed till it was dark almost, and saw the fire grow; and, as it grew darker, appeared more and more; and in corners and upon steeples, and between churches and houses, as far as we could see up the hill of the city, in a most horrid, malicious, bloody flame, not like the fine flame of an ordinary fire …. We stayed till, it being darkish, we saw the fire as one entire arch of fire from this to the other side of the bridge … it made me weep to see it. The churches, houses and all on fire, and flaming at once; and a horrid noise the flames made, and the cracking of the houses at their ruin. So home with a sad heart.'

4. Renaissance Architecture

The Great Fire gave a magnificent opportunity for the rebuilding of London, of which, unfortunately, advantage was not taken. If Wren's plan, embracing wide streets and splendid quays, had been accepted, England would have had the finest capital in Europe. As it was, the houses and streets were put up on the old sites, and a great opportunity for town planning neglected.

At the time of the Fire, the dominant style of architecture was the classical or renaissance style. The classical style, as its name implies, was modelled on the ancient buildings of Greece and Rome; it was reintroduced into Italy at the time of the Renaissance. Italian workmen penetrated into England. An early example of Italian Renaissance work is Henry VII's tomb in Westminster Abbey (1512). Traces of the same style may be seen in many English country houses built during the Tudor period. *English Renaissance Architecture*

In the Stuart period classical architecture came into its own. One of its chief exponents was Inigo Jones (1573-1652), who modelled his style on that of the Italian architect, Palladio. He was employed by both James I and Charles I. For Charles I he designed a new palace at Whitehall, which unfortunately was never completed; but the Banqueting Hall (1619-22), a fine piece of Renaissance work, still remains. Inigo Jones also designed Covent Garden, and had an influence on several country houses. His influence on English architecture was profound. *Inigo Jones 1573-1652*

Sir Christopher Wren (1632-1723), one of England's greatest architects, was born at East Knoyle, in Wiltshire, and was educated at Westminster School and at Wadham College, Oxford. He was made a Fellow of All Souls, and became a Professor of Astronomy and one of the founders with Boyle and others of the Royal Society. He seems to have taken to architecture as an afterthought; but after the Great Fire he was appointed surveyor-general of the royal works, and commissioned to rebuild St. Paul's. *Wren 1632-1723*

St. Paul's Cathedral, Wren's masterpiece, is one of the finest renaissance cathedrals in Europe. The glorious dome, which dominates the city of London, rises over the stately classical building, fronted with Corinthian columns. The cathedral took thirty-five years to build (1675 to 1710). Wren designed fifty other London churches, of which St. Stephen, Walbrook, St. Mary-le-Bow, Cheapside, and St. Clement Danes, Strand, are perhaps the best known. After London, Wren's best work is to be seen at the two Universities; at Oxford, the Sheldonian Theatre, Queen's College Chapel, and Tom Tower, Christ Church; at Cambridge, Trinity College Library, and *St. Paul's Cathedral* *Oxford and Cambridge*

Emmanuel and Pembroke Chapels. Wren also designed the schoolroom at Winchester (known as 'School'); the Monument (to commemorate the Fire); and large parts of Greenwich Hospital and Hampton Court Palace. Wren's influence – and he lived to be ninety – extended over the rest of the Stuart period and into the Georgian.

Vanbrugh   In Queen Anne's reign Sir John Vanbrugh designed, in a development of the classical style known as the baroque, Blenheim Palace, Woodstock, as a residence for the Duke of Marlborough. All over England men were building similar, though smaller, mansions; and the older English towns can all show Queen Anne houses, usually built of brick, of great charm and beauty.

Forms developed from classical architecture held the field throughout the eighteenth century, when many of the finest houses and public buildings in England were erected and a great deal of the

Spirit of   old residential part of London was built. Old Regent Street, since
the Age   unhappily destroyed, was built by James Nash at the beginning of the nineteenth century, after which the monopoly of the classical style was challenged. The long period during which it was in fashion – from James I to George IV – was the period during which England rose to the rank of a great imperial power. Architecture, it has been said, is the mirror of an age. Just as the Gothic spires, heavenward-pointing, speak to us of the age of faith, so the stately, dignified houses of Carolean and Georgian England remind us of the confident generations of aristocrats who built them.

VII

WILLIAM AND MARY AND ANNE

1. The Revolution Settlement

(a) *In England.*

AFTER the final departure to France of James II on December 23rd 1688, the Prince of Orange issued letters summoning a Convention,[12] which met on 22 January 1689. The Convention was a Parliament which could not be so called because it had not been summoned by a monarch. Its first business was to settle the question who should be King of England. Some of the Whigs claimed that James had broken 'the original contract between King and people', but the Tories, with a majority in the Lords, still clung to the theory that Kings were divinely appointed. Some of them wanted to keep James as nominal King while appointing a Regent. Most, however, were prepared to agree that James, having 'violated the fundamental laws and withdrawn himself out of the kingdom, hath abdicated the government and the throne is thereby become vacant.' The Tory Lord Nottingham proposed that the Crown should go to Mary, James' elder daughter, with her husband, William of Orange, acting as Regent. This arrangement would have preserved the principle of hereditary succession, assuming that James' recently born son was not really his at all. But here William intervened; he would have the Crown or nothing – otherwise he would return to Holland. It was then decided to

The Convention Act 1689

Accession of William and Mary 1689

---

[12] So called because not summoned by the Sovereign. (Compare the Convention of 1660.)

WILLIAM III (1650-1702) AND MARY II (1662-1694)
1647 portrait by Gerard van Honthorst

offer the Crown to William and Mary as joint sovereigns, and this offer was accepted in February 1689.[13]

The Bill of Rights 1689

The offer of the Crown was accompanied by a Declaration of Rights, which became the Bill of Rights when passed by the first Parliament of the new reign (1689). The passing of the Bill of Rights was a significant landmark in the long struggle which had been going on between King and Parliament all through the reigns of the Stuart kings. William and Mary were offered, and accepted, the throne on Parliament's terms. The Bill of Rights also limited the Sovereign's power in certain important directions:

1. The 'pretended power' of suspending the laws by royal authority was declared to be illegal and so was the power of exempting individuals from the provisions of the laws (the dispensing power) as it has been exercised of late. In this way, Parliament's legislative supremacy was guaranteed.[14]
2. The king should levy no taxes, except as granted by Parliament.

---

[13] Descent of William and Mary from Charles I:

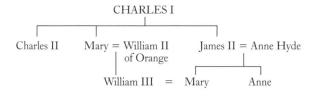

[14] While the 'suspending power' (i.e. suspending a law altogether) was abolished, the 'dispensing power' (i.e. issuing dispensations to particular persons exempting them from the provisions of the law) was condemned 'as it hath been used of late'. This referred to James II's dispensations to Roman Catholics and Nonconformists.

3. The king should not keep a standing army in time of peace without consent of Parliament.[15]

4. Parliament should be free in its electing, and in its subjects of debate, and 'ought to be held frequently'.

The Bill was designed to outlaw some of the measures of James II, such as his attempt to pack Parliament and his maintenance of a large army on Hounslow Heath, but since it was a compromise between Whigs and Tories, it left the Monarchy with most of its powers intact. The King continued to determine policy, to appoint ministers of his own choosing, to veto legislation and to decide when Parliament should be summoned and dissolved. Nonetheless, since 1688 Parliament has met every single year and there was never to be a royal despotism in England. Parliament's decision to grant William III an inadequate income was one reason for this outcome, but more important was the fact that acceptance of William as King committed the country to long wars with Louis XIV. These could be financed only by means of heavy Parliamentary taxation.

The Parliamentary basis of the Monarchy was further underlined when it was declared by Parliament that the King of England could not be a Roman Catholic or marry a person of that religion.

Toleration Act 1689

This 'Glorious Revolution' (1688-9), which determined the future political history of England, was accompanied by a step forward on the path of religious toleration. In order to prevent the Dissenters from accepting James II's offer of toleration, the Anglicans had been compelled to promise a degree of toleration. In addition, as a Calvinist, William of Orange refused to permit the continued persecution of Dissenters. By the Toleration Act (1689), Nonconformist congregations were allowed to worship in their own

---

[15] Mutiny Acts (now called Army Acts), allowing the king to keep an army for one year only, have been passed nearly every year since 1689.

way, without interference from the law. They continued, however, to be barred by the Corporation Act from a share in local government and by the Test Act[16] from any part in national government. These Acts remained unrepealed until the nineteenth century. Roman Catholics were not included in the Toleration Act, but in practice they were allowed to hold their own services in peace.

The Toleration Act was the work of King William, of the Whigs in Parliament, and of the more moderate Churchmen. There was, however, a considerable body of 'High Churchmen' who refused not only to accept the principles of toleration, but even to accept William as King. Six of the seven bishops who had refused to issue James II's Declaration of Indulgence[17] now refused to take the oath to King William (hence they were called Non-Jurors), and they were followed by 400 of the clergy. They were therefore deprived of their sees and benefices, and formed a separate sect of their own, which lasted for some decades. Their departure paved the way for the promotion of 'Low Churchmen', who disliked all forms of religious fanaticism, and who became the typical English church dignitaries of the eighteenth century. *The Non-Jurors*

William III was never loved in England. Unlike his uncle, Charles II, he did not understand the art of making himself personally popular – and he would have scorned to do so even if he had. He knew quite well that his presence in England was regarded as a disagreeable necessity, but he did not allow the fact to interfere with his plans, even when criticism rose to a crescendo in the years 1697-1701. He was a man of integrity and singleness of purpose whose motto *Je maintiendrai* might be translated *I will hold fast*. A greater contrast with Charles II could not easily be imagined. The affection *Character of William III*

---

[16] See above, p. 90. It was the Tories who insisted, against the wishes of the king and the Whigs, in retaining these Acts on the Statute Book. But annual indemnity acts were soon passed.

[17] See above, p. 99

which William failed, or scorned, to inspire among his subjects was given to his kind-hearted wife, Mary, who died in 1694, and for whose funeral Henry Purcell, England's revered composer, wrote the most sublime music of the Baroque period.

William and
English
politicians

The main object of William's life, in pursuit of which he had accepted the Crown of England, was to overthrow the power of Louis XIV. The first eight years of his reign in England were spent in a war against France. William used the power of England as a means to accomplish his European aims; beyond that he had little interest in this country. He did not trust English politicians, and with good reason, for nearly all of them – Whigs as well as Tories – kept in touch with the Court of St. Germain, where James II lived. They regarded William as a stop-gap, and always bore in mind that another turn of Fortune's wheel might bring back the exiled James. In any case, English ministers and diplomats lacked the experience needed to manage foreign and military business for the King. William, therefore, had perforce to give his chief confidence to Huguenots (French Protestants) and to his own Dutchmen, and particularly to William Bentinck, whom he made Earl of Portland.

The King himself was at the head of the government, and he kept the direction of foreign affairs entirely in his own hands. But, since he was dependent on Parliament both for men and money, he had to work with English politicians. The government was not then formed, as it is now, generally from the party which could command a majority in the House of Commons. William chose his first ministers from both parties; many of them were Whigs, but the chief minister was a Tory – Danby, Charles II's old Treasurer, now elevated to the earldom of Carmarthen. As the war proceeded, however, William found that he needed a more united and coherent ministry and he turned to a group of Whig ministers known as the Junto. They alone possessed the realism and courage to adopt the unpopular financial measures that were needed to wage war successfully. They did not forget that, if England lost the war, the restoration of James II by French arms was a probability.

It was to guard against any such restoration of the old Stuart line that Parliament passed the Act of Settlement in 1701. Since Queen Mary was dead, the heir to William's throne had been declared in the Bill of Rights to be his sister-in-law, the Princess Anne. The Act of Settlement now declared that if Anne should die without direct heirs,[18] as seemed likely after the death of her only surviving son in 1700, the Crown should pass to the Dowager Electress of Hanover, a Protestant grand-daughter of James I, and her descendants.[19] The Act of Settlement, which thus ensured the succession of the House of Hanover and has given England her present royal line, excluded James II (who died the same year) and his son from the throne. It was passed at a time when a further struggle between England and Louis XIV was about to break out.

Act of Settlement 1701

(b) *In Scotland.*

The results of the Revolution were no less important in Scotland. Scots had played a significant role in encouraging and assisting William's invasion of England in 1688.Though James II imagined his regime in Scotland strong enough to risk removing his Scottish army to help his cause in England, he was rapidly proved wrong. By early December James II's Scottish ministers were in flight as anti-Catholic demonstrations swept the country. The main difference from the situation in England was the determination of large numbers of Scots not only to undo what James II had done, but also to change the religious settlement established at the Restoration of Charles II. Particularly in south-west Scotland, many Episcopalian clergymen (those supporting government of the Church by bishops) were ejected from their parishes by local Presbyterians. When the

---

[18] Anne had had a large family; but her only remaining child, the Duke of Gloucester, had just died (1700).

[19] For note 19 see next page.

Convention was elected and met in Edinburgh, it turned out to be dominated by Presbyterians.

The Convention passed a resolution called the 'Claim of Right', corresponding to the Declaration of Rights in England. James VII (James II of England), the last of the long line of Stuart kings of Scotland, was declared to have forfeited the Crown, which was offered to William and Mary. Henceforth, the monarchy in Scotland was to be subject to limitations similar to those imposed on it in 1688-9 in England. In Scotland, however, government of the Church by bishops was abolished and Presbyterian ministers turned out of their parishes since 1661 were reinstated. In their hour of victory, the Presbyterians wanted more still. William III hoped to make the Scottish church comprehensive, but the Presbyterians seized every opportunity to deprive Episcopalians of their posts until by 1720 the Presbyterians had secured a monopoly of the churches. As a result, Scottish society remained deeply divided in religion: whereas under the Restoration governments the Presbyterians had been persecuted and resentful, after 1688 the Episcopalians felt downtrodden. There

19

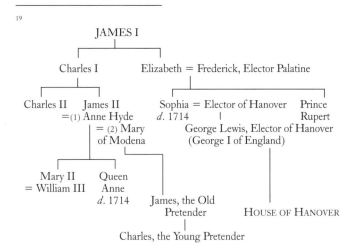

were many Scots who had reason to regret the Revolution of 1688 and to hope for its undoing.

Unlike in England, the new regime in Scotland faced a significant challenge from Jacobites, that is those who wished to bring back James II or his son James, the Old Pretender. In 1689 a rebellion was launched from the Highlands by John Graham of Claverhouse, Viscount Dundee. Even though he succeeded in collecting only 2,000 men, 'Bonny Dundee' won a battle over the government forces of General Mackay in the Pass of Killiecrankie in 1689, but he himself fell in the hour of victory. Without his leadership, Mackay's superior forces were bound to prevail, as they did by 1690.

Battle of Killiecrankie 1689

After this the Highlanders were compelled to come to terms. It was agreed that all the clans should take the oath of allegiance by the first day of the year 1692. All did so except the chief of the Macdonalds of Glencoe, who was delayed by accident. Sir John Dalrymple, a Secretary of State, induced William (who was in Holland) to punish the clan – 'to extirpate that sept (clan) of thieves'! One hundred and twenty men of Argyll's regiment under Robert Campbell of Glenlyon were chosen as the instruments of punishment, and were sent to the Glencoe valley, where for a fortnight they were entertained as guests. One morning they treacherously rose up and attacked their hosts: the chief and thirty-seven of his clan were butchered – the rest escaped to the hills. The responsibility for this savage deed must be attributed partly to the customary feuds of the Highland chiefs and partly to the Government. The Jacobites denounced the crime at home and abroad.

Massacre of Glencoe 1693

In the twenty years after 1688 the Scottish economy was in a very depressed state. Traditional trades with France, Holland and the Baltic were dislocated by the wars against Louis XIV and the Great Northern War of 1700-21. Exports to England were hampered by English tariffs. Scottish agriculture was carried on by primitive methods and the terrible weather of the 1690s had led to famines and depopulation in some areas. There was one serious effort to develop the economy in a fresh direction, but it was to prove a demoralizing failure. Several London merchants formed a plan for promoting Scottish colonization in Africa or the Indies; the plan was enthusiastically taken up in Edinburgh, where the Scottish Parliament passed a Bill setting up the Company of Scotland Trading to Africa and the Indies (1695). But the English Parliament, jealous for the monopoly of the East India Company, was hostile, whereupon the London Scottish merchants grew alarmed and dropped the scheme. But the Edinburgh merchants persisted, and large sums of money were subscribed in Scotland, in what amounted to a national effort to promote Scottish colonization. Darien, near Panama, was eventually chosen as the place for a colony; it was intended to establish an overland trade-route across the isthmus, connecting the Atlantic and Pacific. But it was an unfortunate choice, for the Spaniards were bound to object, and King William was then conducting delicate negotiations on the future of the Spanish Empire.[20] It was impossible for him to countenance the Darien colony or to defend an enterprise undertaken against his wishes. Three expeditions were, however, sent out (1698-9); all ended in disaster, and the would-be colonists were at last forced, owing to Spanish hostility and the bad climate, to give up the enterprise. The shareholders lost practically all the money they had invested. They blamed England for the failure of the enterprise and by the turn of the century relations beween England and Scotland were extremely hostile.

The Revolution of 1688 had made the Scottish Parliament largely free from royal control. The Parliaments of William's and Anne's reigns proved very obstructive and some of their measures were ominous. At Westminster the Act of Settlement was passed, but the Scottish Parliament passed no such act. The Scots accepted Anne as Queen, but it was by no means certain that they would accept the

---

[20] See below, p. 157

Hanoverians.[21] As long as the Parliament remained independent of Westminster, it was free to pass its own laws, and the Act of Security of 1703 specifically laid it down that Anne's successor should be a descendant of the Stuarts different from the choice made by England, unless England made acceptable concessions. A further Act involved arming the people of the border counties, a measure that seemed to envisage a future war with England. The Westminster Parliament responded to these provocations with the Aliens Act of 1705 empowering Anne to appoint commissioners to negotiate a union of the two Parliaments, provided that the Scots did the same. Yet there was also a threat: if the Act of Security remained in force, then Scots would be declared aliens in England, incapable of owning or inheriting land, and most Scottish imports would be excluded.

By now it was clear that the alternatives were full union or a war between the two countries that could only be to the advantage of France. After long negotiations, the Act of Union was passed (1707) both at London and Edinburgh, and the Scottish Parliament came to an end. The Scots were allowed 45 members in the Commons and 16 peers in the Lords in the United Parliament of Great Britain. They were also allowed to keep their own Kirk and their own law courts. Free trade between the two countries was established.

The Union was not at once popular. Bribery was necessary to secure the passage of the legislation through the Edinburgh Parliament and there were violent mob protests in the Scottish capital. The English complained that under the agreement the Scots paid too little tax and had too many MPs. Yet the Union survived. Gradually, the Scots were won over by the economic benefits: the British empire was to be an Anglo-Scottish empire and Glasgow in

The Act of Union 1707

---

[21] In 1703 the Scottish Parliament passed a Security Act, claiming the right to choose their own sovereign – not necessarily the same person as the English sovereign – on the death of Anne.

time became a great imperial city. The English were looking mainly for political benefits and especially a guarantee against a revival of the Auld Alliance of Scotland and France which had repeatedly menaced England till the reign of Queen Elizabeth. The Jacobite cause did not immediately wither, but the only major Jacobite invasion of Anne's reign, in 1708, mustered little support and proved a fiasco.

(c) *In Ireland.*

The Revolution, called 'Glorious' in England, was given no such name in Ireland. Here the Catholic majority made a great effort to undo the results of English successes against Irish revolts in the 1590s and after 1641. They hoped to achieve this by throwing in their lot with the Catholic James II. James landed at Kinsale in March 1689 and summoned a Parliament, which gave the Irish Catholics free exercise of their religion and undid the Cromwellian land settlement, which had been only modified at the Restoration, by giving landholders of 1641 or their heirs the right to recover their lands. Had this legislation been made effective, a new ruling class would have been established in Ireland and the Anglo-Protestant ascendancy would have been overturned. Resistance to this Catholic revolution was strongest in Ulster, where large numbers of Protestants had settled in the reign of James I. The Orangemen – as the Ulster supporters of William of Orange were called – defended Londonderry after James had overrun the rest of the country. The siege of Londonderry lasted fifteen weeks and the inhabitants were reduced to living upon dogs, cats, rats and mice. But at last in July 1689 an English ship broke the boom which had been placed across the River Foyle, and supplies were brought in.

Next year in 1690 William III landed in Ireland. His multi-national army defeated James' numerically inferior army composed largely of Irish Catholics and Frenchmen at the Battle of the Boyne on July 1,1690. The fighting was not heavy and the losses on both

Margin notes:
- James II in Ireland
- Siege of Londonderry 1689
- Battle of the Boyne

sides were small, but William's victory proved decisive because of James' reaction. He was one of the first to quit the field and immediately took ship for France, showing no more determination in defence of his Irish kingdom than he had two years earlier in defence of his English one. Deserted by their King after the first blow had been struck, the Irish were left to the doubtful mercy of William's generals. Irish hopes were effectively extinguished at the disastrous battle of Aughrim in July 1691. The last town to hold out was Limerick, defended by Patrick Sarsfield until the autumn of 1691. Then a treaty was signed by which the defenders agreed to surrender Limerick on condition that the Irish Catholics should enjoy as much liberty as they had done under Charles II.

Siege of Limerick 1691

The liberties for Irish Catholics promised under the Treaty of Limerick, limited though they were, seemed too dangerous to many Protestants both in England and in Ireland. The only way of preventing fresh Irish rebellions seemed to be to impose further restrictions on Catholics. In 1691 the English Parliament passed a law that only Protestants could sit in the Irish Parliament. This body had become much more important, because William needed the taxes it granted. It used its power to pass a series of harsh penal laws, some brought in under William and Mary, and others under Queen Anne. By these laws Catholics were forbidden to sit on juries; they could not serve in the army, or on town councils, or enter the teaching or legal professions. No Catholic bishops or monks were allowed in Ireland and no new Catholic clergy could enter the country. Catholics could not buy land, and when one of the existing Catholic landowners died, his property did not descend to his heir, but had to be split up among all his children. The proportion of land held by Catholics had already been reduced by confiscations from those who had supported James II: by 1703 only 14% of profitable land was in Catholic hands (down from 22% in 1688). The incentive for landowners to convert to Protestantism was so great that this percentage appears to have fallen to 5% by 1760.

The Penal and Commercial Laws

The Protestant minority in Ireland was genuinely afraid of a repetition of the Catholic Rebellion of 1641, or of the Civil War of 1689, especially while the continuing war with Catholic France kept alive the possibility of French help for Irish Catholic rebels. But even the Protestants of Ulster, who had fought for King William, were kept in a subordinate position. Most of them were Dissenters, whose numbers were much increased by the immigration into Ulster in the 1690s of perhaps 50,000 Scots. The Anglican landowners and clergy feared a challenge to their dominant position in Ireland and welcomed restrictions on office-holding by Dissenters imposed in Anne's reign. Free exercise of their religion was fully guaranteed to Irish Dissenters in 1719, but the ascendancy of the Anglican Church of Ireland was to remain unchallenged till the 19th century.

The Anglican landowners of Ireland, however, were kept in subordination to the English Parliament and therefore to English interests. One effect of this subordination was the tightening of the commercial regulations designed to favour English economic interests at Ireland's expense. The Irish cattle trade had already been ruined by an Act of Charles II's Parliament;[22] now it was the turn of the Irish wool trade. The export of wool to any country except England was prohibited, and from England the wool was largely kept out by high tariffs, provisions which benefited English wool-growers. Effectively, Ireland was an English colony, its dependent status underlined by the growing habit of appointing Englishmen to Irish offices in Church and state.

---

[22] See above, Chap. V

2. William III and Louis XIV

The ambitions of Louis XIV form the central theme of European history in the second half of the seventeenth century. Louis had, in the course of a long series of wars, seized large slices of the Spanish Netherlands and nearly ruined Holland by his invasion of 1672. His further designs threatened both Holland and Germany. Already, by the seizure of the city of Strasbourg in 1681, the French frontier had reached the Rhine; Louis' troops had earlier occupied Lorraine. The Emperor Leopold and the German princes were seriously alarmed; they formed an alliance known as the League of Augsburg in 1686, with the object of opposing any further French advance eastward. This alliance was joined by William of Orange, as Stadtholder of Holland, before he became King of England.

The European situation was entirely altered by the Revolution in England which overthrew James II and set William and Mary on the throne. The long English subservience to France, which had lasted for twenty years under Charles II, and his brother, was broken at last. Instead of the Stuarts, Louis was confronted with the first statesman in Europe seated now on the English throne; William of Orange was at last in a position to face his arch-enemy on equal terms. Part of Louis' object in fighting the Anglo-Dutch-German combination was therefore to dethrone William and restore James. It was this fact that made the English fight for their little-loved King.

King William stood at the head of the European alliance against France, England, Holland, and Spain leagued with the Emperor and the German princes. This War of the League of Augsburg lasted eight years (1689-97). It was fought on all the French frontiers, at sea, in Ireland, and in the colonies of North America. To begin with, England came close to losing the war. James II enjoyed initial success in Ireland and William was worried enough to go there himself in 1690, when he won decisively at the Boyne. 1690 was also a year of naval defeat, when Admiral Herbert, in command of the Anglo-

The ambitions of Louis XIV

League of Augsburg 1686

Effects of the English Revolution

War of the League of Augsburg 1689-97

Dutch fleet, was worsted in the Channel by the French, who fortunately failed to exploit their victory. In 1692 Louis hoped to build on this success and prepared a fleet to invade England; James II went down to Cape La Hogue to embark with it. But the numerically superior Dutch and English fleets – the English under Admiral Russell – scattered the French in the Channel; the battle of Barfleur ended all chance of an invasion of England. For the rest of the war French commerce suffered severely from English and Dutch attacks. Not for the first or the last time, the command of the sea safeguarded England against invasion. Yet it was not enough to decide the outcome of the European war.

Battle of
Barfleur
1692

Next to the command of the sea, England's most important object was to secure control of the Low Countries. It has always been one of the cardinal principles of English policy to prevent the Low Countries – Holland and Belgium – from falling into the hands of a hostile power. For this object the British fought later on against the First French Republic and Napoleon; for this object they fought the Germans in the First World War. In 1689 both England and Holland were determined that Louis XIV should not conquer the Spanish Netherlands (modern Belgium). King William therefore crossed to the Spanish Netherlands year after year, and fought a series of campaigns against the French generals. English soldiers fought in the Flanders mud as their ancestors had done under Henry V and as their descendants were to do under George V. The French won several battles, but William was always skilful enough to retreat with most of his army intact. His principal success was the capture of the fortress of Namur (1695).

The Low
Countries

It was the waging of King William's war against Louis XIV which brought about a financial revolution in English history. One of the main causes of the former quarrels between English Kings and their Parliaments had been the question of taxation. Since war is always more expensive than peace, war had always meant fresh taxation. The statesmen of the Whig Junto, Sir John Somers and Charles

The War and
the National
Debt

Montagu, now hit upon the plan of making posterity pay for wars. The National Debt, which has been chiefly incurred in waging war, is not a debt which has to be settled by one generation; the banking system which the Whigs began under William III carries the Debt on from one generation to another. The ministry of William III obtained funds – in the first instance, £1,200,000 – by establishing a company to lend money to the Government. This company was the Bank of England, founded in 1694. The Bank at first borrowed money from the public at 2.5 per cent, and lent it to the Government at 8 per cent. This system meant that the government would go on paying for the war long after peace had been made and would therefore remain dependent on parliamentary taxation. This is why monarchs henceforth could never dispense with Parliament. Yet the Bank was not at first popular with many MPs. The Whig Junto seemed enormously to have increased the power of the moneyed interest. The landowners, who were so important in Parliament, resented this power and were appalled at the prospect of high taxation far into the future for the benefit of moneyed men in the City of London.

Founding of the Bank of England 1694

By 1697 both sides in the European conflict were anxious for peace, which was accordingly concluded at Ryswick, near The Hague. For the first time Louis XIV emerged from a war without making any fresh conquests. He agreed to allow the Dutch to maintain garrisons in the Barrier Fortresses (e.g. Namur, Ypres, Menin) in the Spanish Netherlands. He also recognized William III as King of England. In America the English restored Acadie (Nova Scotia) to the French in return for Fort Albany which the French had taken from the Hudson's Bay Company.

Treaty of Ryswick 1697

No sooner was this peace concluded than Europe was faced with the problem of the succession to the Spanish throne. Charles II of Spain (1665-1700) was the last of the Habsburg kings of Spain and he had no children. The question of the succession to his throne involved large issues – who should be the next King of Spain, and what would happen to the vast Spanish Empire at his death. Charles

The Spanish Succession Question

had two sisters; the elder had married Louis XIV, the younger the
Emperor Leopold I.[23] If either Louis or Leopold should claim to
succeed Charles, the balance of power in Europe would be upset; it
was unthinkable that the union of France and Spain, or of Spain and
Austria, could be brought about without war. Louis and Leopold
were both willing, however, to renounce their claims to the Spanish
Empire in favour of another member of their own family. The
Austrian candidate was the Emperor's younger son, the Archduke
Charles; Louis proposed one of his own grandsons. Another claimant
was Joseph Ferdinand, Electoral Prince of Bavaria; he was by far the
most suitable candidate for he was not in the line of succession to the
Imperial throne.[24] Had he become King of Spain, the succession of
either a French or an Austrian claimant would have been avoided.

---

[23] The elder sister, Louis' wife, had renounced her rights to the Spanish throne at
the time of her marriage. But the French Court questioned whether this
renunciation was binding on her descendants.

[24]

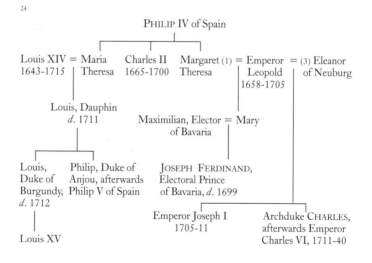

Louis was willing to agree to the Bavarian's taking the Spanish Crown, provided France was given some compensation. He therefore signed the First Partition Treaty (1698) recognizing Joseph Ferdinand as heir to the Spanish throne and its dominions, except Naples and Sicily, which were to go to France. Then, unfortunately, the Electoral Prince died of small-pox (1699).

First Partition Treaty 1698

Louis was not anxious to embark on another war for the sake of the Spanish inheritance. He therefore agreed to a Second Partition Treaty – which William III arranged in the interests of peace – recognizing the Austrian Archduke as heir to Spain; France was to be compensated with Naples and Sicily. But there were two objections to this treaty. First, the Emperor Leopold would not sign it, but claimed the whole Spanish inheritance for his son. Secondly, the Spanish ministers would have none of it; they were determined that the Spanish Empire should not be partitioned, whatever else happened. This determination they now conveyed to the feeble mind of the King of Spain.

Second Partition Treaty 1699

Charles II of Spain had been a semi-imbecile since boyhood. Macaulay, in a well-known passage of his History, has described the last days of this wretched man.

Charles II of Spain

'That he was too weak to lift his food to his misshapen mouth, that, at thirty-seven, he had the bald head and wrinkled face of a man of seventy, that his complexion was turning from yellow to green – these were no longer the worst symptoms of his malady. He had always been afraid of ghosts and demons; and it had long been necessary that three friars should watch every night by his restless bed to guard against hobgoblins. But now he was firmly convinced that he was bewitched, that there was a devil within him, that there were devils all around him.'[25]

---

[25] Macaulay, *History of England*, Chapter XXIV

It was this unfortunate King who was now induced to make a will naming Louis' grandson Philip of Anjou as the inheritor of all his dominions, so that the Spanish Empire should remain undivided. Having done this, he expired (1700).

His Will and Death 1700

The news of Charles' death and will came as a thunderbolt to European statesmen. Louis decided to throw over the agreement made in the Second Partition Treaty, especially as it had not been approved by the Emperor, and to accept the will. The French Court was assembled at Versailles; the King was closeted with his grandson. At length the doors were thrown open; Louis appeared leaning on Philip's arm. '*Messieurs,*' he said, '*voici le roi d'Espagne!*'

Louis accepts the Will

Louis' decision led to war. Neither England nor Austria would permit the whole Spanish Empire to pass to Philip, even though that prince renounced his right to succeed to the French throne. William III was a sick man, but he braced himself for one final effort. He knew that he himself would not live to wage the war which he was preparing; he looked round for a man to take his place. With unerring instinct he chose the one person in England capable of carrying on his task; he chose a man who had long been his personal enemy, and whom he had often suspected of treason against him – John Churchill, Earl of Marlborough. Marlborough was the chief adherent of the heiress to the throne, the Princess Anne, whose bosom friend was Sarah Churchill, Marlborough's wife. Anne and Lady Marlborough hated King William, whom they always referred to as 'Mr. Caliban', though since Queen Mary's death they had become more reconciled to him. William now showed, against all expectation, that he trusted Marlborough. He sent him as English minister to Holland, charged with the task of forming a Grand Alliance with the Dutch and the Emperor against France. Marlborough succeeded in his task. His wonderful charm of manner well fitted him for the task of ambassador; he stepped into the place William had prepared for him as the chief representative of England. In September 1701 the Treaty of the Grand Alliance was signed, and William's purpose was accomplished.

William III and Marlborough

Treaty of the Grand Alliance 1701

A week later James II died at St. Germain. Louis immediately recognized his son (known to English history as the Old Pretender) as James III of England. It was a foolish act, for it united England against him. Parliament had already settled the Crown on Anne,[26] and after her (through the Act of Settlement) on the House of Hanover; and Englishmen were not going to allow Louis XIV to dictate to them who their King should be. Besides, Louis' actions were most alarming; his troops had occupied the Spanish Netherlands and driven the Dutch garrisons from the Barrier Fortresses, a measure justified as upholding the authority of Louis' grandson Philip, the new King of Spain. English commercial interests were upset as measures were taken which harmed English trade with Spain and its empire and presaged exploitation by French merchants of the Spanish territories of the New World. War became inevitable. Just before it broke out, William died. While he was out riding, his horse stumbled and threw him, and he broke his collarbone. A chill followed – more than the feeble frame of the sick King could endure. His passing was unmourned, for he had not been loved in England, though he had ousted an unpopular King. He died, and Anne succeeded – as the roll of Marlborough's drums heralded what was, up till then, the greatest war in British history.

Death of James II 1701

Death of William III 1702

3. Marlborough

Queen Anne, the younger daughter of James II and Anne Hyde, was the last of the Stuart sovereigns of England. She was an unsophisticated, pious woman, married to a nonentity, Prince George of Denmark. She had been the mother of a large family, but all her children, except one who had reached the age of twelve, had died in

Queen Anne

---

[26] See above, p. 149

infancy. Her reign, despite military success on a scale unknown since the middle ages, was not a happy time for Anne herself, for she lived the life of an invalid, and was seldom free from pain.

For the greater part of her reign Anne was completely under the Marlborough influence of the Churchills – Marlborough and his sharp-tempered wife. The duke, as he became in 1702, was now over fifty, but only on the threshold of his great career. The son of a West-country squire, Sir Winston Churchill, he had won a name for himself in the witty, heartless court of Charles II. But his marriage to Sarah Jennings was a love match; Marlborough and his duchess were a devoted couple, and the duke's first action after the battle of Blenheim was to pen a hasty note to his faithful Sarah. From the time when William III used him to construct the Grand Alliance against Louis XIV till 1710 Marlborough was in charge of British diplomacy. In 1702 he became also captain-general of the allied armies. To his men Marlborough was all that a general should be: he looked after their wellbeing and was especially insistent on the best possible treatment of the wounded. He led them in battles, which he knew how to win. His soldiers loved 'Corporal John', but politicians were not so grateful. The duke's charm of manner was no shield against political hatred and, when once his enemies had undermined his influence with the Queen, it proved easy to ruin him.

The head of the war ministry was Sidney, Lord Godolphin, a close Godolphin personal friend and relation of the duke. Godolphin became Lord Treasurer, and was for eight years (1702-10) Prime Minister in all but name. He was more of an administrator than a politician, but he had to secure the men and money essential for the conduct of the war. This meant managing the bitterly divided party politicians of the House of Commons. Till 1708 he was able to work with Robert Harley, by now a Tory, but a moderate one. Harley's value to

---

[27] Godolphin's son Francis married Henrietta Churchill, the duke's elder daughter.

QUEEN ANNE (1665-1714, REIGN: 1702-14) WITH HER SON WILLIAM, DUKE OF
GLOUCESTER (1689-1700)
(Portrait c. 1694 by Sir Godfrey Kneller)

Godolphin was his ability to get the ministry's vital war legislation
through Parliament.

The War of the Spanish Succession, on which Great Britain was
now embarking, was fought on four fronts – in Europe, in America,
in the Atlantic and in the Mediterranean. In this war France and
Spain were close allies. French armies occupied the Spanish
Netherlands and accompanied Louis' grandson to Spain, where he

War of the
Spanish
Succession
1702-13

was enthroned as Philip V. The war in Europe may be divided into four theatres of operations: the conquest of the Spanish Netherlands by Marlborough; the attempt of the French to subdue south Germany and reach Vienna; the fighting in north Italy, where the Duke of Savoy joined the allies; and the attempt of the allies to wrest Spain from Philip V.

When Marlborough took command in 1702, the French were in possession of the whole of the Spanish Netherlands. The Anglo-Dutch army faced them, and Marlborough began his attack. His operations in the first two years (1702-3) were along the rivers Meuse and Rhine; he held the line of the Rhine as far as Bonn, but did not advance far into the Spanish Netherlands. Meanwhile the Emperor was in a precarious position; his Hungarian subjects were in revolt,[28] and his great general, Prince Eugène, had been defeated by the French in Italy. Worse still, the French had persuaded the Elector of Bavaria to join them, and were preparing to march through south Germany to Vienna.

Campaign of 1704
The Emperor appealed to Marlborough, who, seeing that Austria must be saved if the war was to be won, decided to withdraw the bulk of his forces from the Rhine to the Danube. The decision was a huge gamble: Marlborough needed a quick and decisive victory against an enemy whose last serious defeat had been in the 1630s, for he could not leave the Dutch exposed to Louis' armies in the Netherlands for long. In June and July 1704 he moved by swift marches across Germany; the French had begun their march through Bavaria. On the night of 12 August Marlborough lay at Munster, on the Danube, in command of a mixed army of English (10,000), Dutch, and German troops. He had joined forces with the Imperial army under

---

[28] The Emperor had recently conquered Hungary from the Turks. The Austrians won the battle of Mohacs (1687), and the Turks later surrendered Hungary by treaty (1699). Hungary was ruled by the Hapsburg monarchs till 1918.

Prince Eugène; the combined allied forces numbered 52,000. The French and Bavarians, who were superior to their opponents in numbers of men and cannon, were encamped behind the marshes of the little brook Nebel, which flows into the Danube at Blindheim, or Blenheim, as the Allies called it. The French commander, Marshal Tallard, thought himself secure; his right flank rested on the Danube, his left on a forest. He did not imagine that Marlborough would dare to attack him by crossing the marshes of the Nebel.

The battle of Blenheim began the next day (13 August 1704) on a front four miles long. Marlborough waited all the morning for Prince Eugène to get into position opposite the French left; in the meantime his own men were constructing bridges to cross the Nebel. Then, in the afternoon, they crossed. Tallard mistakenly failed to attack while they were still disorganized from crossing the brook and he also committed far too many men to the defence of the village of Blenheim. Marlborough's forces surrounded it, thereby excluding a large number of French soldiers from the fighting in the centre where the battle would be decided. The determination and resourcefulness of Prince Eugène were vital in checking the numerically superior French forces opposite him and his close relationship with Marlborough proved important when he sent aid to the latter who was temporarily under severe threat in the centre. Yet it was the success of Marlborough's cavalry in the centre that turned the battle into a decisive victory. The French centre gave way. Except for the Bavarians on the left, who retired in good order, the retreat became a rout; the French fled in headlong confusion, and hundreds were drowned in the Danube. Marshal Tallard himself was taken prisoner. Finally, the defenders of Blenheim village surrendered and 10,000 prisoners were captured. The results of Blenheim were overwhelming. Marlborough had won the greatest English victory since Agincourt; he had humbled the pride of Louis' famous army, saved Vienna, and cleared Germany of the French. Yet his losses were heavy. Casualties numbered about 12,500, one fifth of them British.

Battle of Bleinheim 13 August 1704

After pursuing the French across the Rhine, Marlborough
returned to the Netherlands, where he fought six campaigns in the
following six years. The campaign of 1706 was another great
triumph. He won the battle of Ramillies and occupied Antwerp and
Brussels. In 1708 he surprised the French at Oudenarde and drove
them across the frontier. Lille fell, and the road to Paris seemed open.
The next year (1709) he beat the enemy, though at great cost, at
Malplaquet, and took Mons. But the French resistance was
hardening; they had lost the Spanish Netherlands, but they were still
capable of defending their own frontier.

The Belgian
campaigns

Meanwhile the allies had carried the war into Spain itself. A week
before Blenheim, Sir George Rooke, in command of an English fleet,
appeared off Gibraltar. The fortress had been left practically
unguarded; a few English sailors climbed the Rock, and Gibraltar
surrendered. This was an English success of great importance for
the future; the command of the Straits of Gibraltar gave the British
the entry into the Mediterranean and was the foundation of their later
dominance there. In 1708 this success was followed up by the capture
of Minorca, one of the Balearic Islands.

Capture of
Gibraltar
1704

and of
Minorca
1708

Two years after the fall of Gibraltar a British expedition under the
Earl of Peterborough, accompanied by the Archduke Charles, passed
through the Straits and sailed up the Spanish coast. A landing was
made near Barcelona; the city was stormed and taken in 1705. In
Catalonia the allies were helped by Catalan separatism, but no such
help was available in Castile, which stood resolutely against 'Charles
III', as the Archduke called himself. Under the Duke of Berwick,[29]
an illegitimate son of James II, French and Castilian forces
completely routed the allies at the battle of Almanza (1707). The
allied attempt to impose on the Spanish people a sovereign not of

The War in
Spain

[29] Berwick was one of the ablest generals in the French service. He was an
illegitimate son of James II and Arabella Churchill, Marlborough's sister.

their own choice was failing, but the British government had convinced itself that the attempt could not be abandoned, since French power would be too overwhelming if a French prince were allowed to be King of Spain.

Battle of Almanza 1707

4. Queen Anne and the Tories

The final stages of the War of the Spanish Succession, and the events leading up to a general peace, were determined by a change which took place in the government of England.

Godolphin's Government, which supplied Marlborough with money for the war, became in time a ministry entirely dependent upon the Whigs. But the dismissal in 1708 of the Tory ministers, Robert Harley and Henry St. John, proved to be the undoing of the Government. Both these men were ambitious and skilful, and they plotted the overthrow of Godolphin and Marlborough. Harley had a cousin, Mrs. Masham, whom he introduced into the royal circle with the object of undermining the influence of the Duchess of Marlborough. Mrs Masham's influence on the Queen is often exaggerated. Several other factors had began to alienate the Queen from the ministry. She disliked Whig religious and political principles and she had increasing doubts about the foreign policy associated with Marlborough, Godolphin and the Whigs. Their policy can be summed up as 'no peace without Spain', a policy which promised war without end, since the Spaniards were plainly determined to stick by Philip V and the allies lacked the power to eject him from Spain.

Harley and St. John in opposition

Then, in 1710, a political storm arose over a sermon preached in St. Paul's Cathedral by Dr. Sacheverell. This high church clergyman attacked the ministers and the bishops they had appointed as 'false brethren' who were destroying the Church for the benefit of the Dissenters. He appeared to question the principle of religious toleration and even the legitimacy of the Revolution of 1688. The

Dr. Sacheverell

Whig ministry decided to impeach Sacheverell. Immediately the cry

Fall of the Godolphin Ministry 1710

'The Church in danger' was raised; riotous London mobs and Tory pamphlet writers combined to attack, in their different ways, the now unpopular ministry. Sacheverell was condemned by a small majority of the House of Lords, and sentenced merely to three years suspension from preaching. Such a sentence was almost as good as an acquittal, and the doctor's supporters went wild with delight.

Encouraged by the temper of the public, Harley decided to strike at his enemies. He persuaded the Queen to dismiss Godolphin and the Whigs; she did so and Harley became Prime Minister in effect (though the name was not yet in general use).[30] A general election was then held (1710) and a large Tory majority was returned. Harley was made Earl of Oxford, and St. John, his right-hand man, became Lord Bolingbroke.

The Oxford Ministry 1710-14

The first business of the Tories was to make peace. The war had become a stalemate, and the Tories refused to continue it merely in order to retain Marlborough in power and enable him to win yet more military glory. They reckoned that war was being prolonged for the benefit of Whig financiers in the City of London and at the expense of Tory landowners who had to pay heavy taxes, especially the hated land tax. The Queen was inclined to back the Tories: she was growing tired of the duchess (Mrs Freeman, as Anne called her) and her tempers; the star of Mrs. Masham was in the ascendant. There was certainly a great deal to be said in favour of peace, especially when, in 1711, the Emperor Joseph I died. His successor was his brother, the Archduke Charles, who became the Emperor Charles VI. There was clearly no purpose in continuing the war in order to make Charles King of Spain, and so unite Spain and Austria, as in the days of Charles V. The allies had failed to dislodge Philip V from Spain itself, though they had conquered the Spanish provinces in

---

[30] The name Prime Minister was occasionally used in Anne's reign in reference to Godolphin. Defoe, writing in 1714, twice speaks of Oxford as Prime Minister.

Italy and the Netherlands. These points were made clear by the publication (in 1711) of Dean Swift's famous pamphlet, *The Conduct of the Allies*.

The Conduct of the Allies 1711

Dean Swift was a Tory, and his virulent pen was at the service of the ministry. Swift is now best remembered as the author of *Gulliver's Travels*, but in his own day he was known and feared as a political writer. The publication of the *Conduct of the Allies* was his greatest triumph; it did much to procure the dismissal of the great Duke of Marlborough. Never in British history has so much literary talent been put to political uses as in the days of Queen Anne. Richard Steele, an ex-army officer, was an Irishman like Swift; he became a Whig pamphleteer and founder of the *Tatler* (1709) and *The Spectator* (1710). *The Spectator* was published daily; its most distinguished contributor was Joseph Addison, a man who had a great influence in the development of English prose and the creator of Sir Roger de Coverley. Another writer of genius was Daniel Defoe,[31] of whom it has been said that he changed his politics as often as the Queen changed her ministries. Such was the array of talent placed before the readers of Queen Anne's day when they opened their daily newspapers in their coffee-houses.

Political writers under Queen Anne

The Spectator 1710

Even before Marlborough was dismissed in 1711, Oxford and Bolingbroke opened negotiations for peace with France behind his back, and behind the backs of their allies. The Duke of Ormonde, who succeeded Marlborough in command, had the humiliation of being obliged to order his troops to desert their old ally, Prince Eugène, in the hour of battle – for Oxford had already come to terms with the French. The other allies eventually came in, and a general peace was arranged at Utrecht in 1713.

Dismissal of Marlborough 1711

The Treaty of Utrecht is one of the great landmarks in British and European history. From it Britain emerged as a front-ranking

The Treaty of Utrecht 1712

---

[31] For *Robinson Crusoe* (1719), see Volume V (1714-1837).

European power. Her old enemy, King Louis XIV, was humbled, for his career of conquest was at an end, and France was nearly bankrupt. The principal terms of the settlement were as follows:

1. The Allies acknowledged Philip V as King of Spain and of the Indies, on the understanding that he was to be excluded from the succession to the French throne.

2. Louis XIV threw over the Pretender, James III, and recognized the Protestant Succession in Great Britain.

3. The King of Spain resigned the Spanish Netherlands, Milan, Sardinia, and Naples to the Emperor, and Sicily to the Duke of Savoy.

Gibraltar, Minorca, and New-foundland

4. Britain received Gibraltar and Minorca in Europe, Acadie (Nova Scotia) in North America, and the French gave up their claims to Hudson Bay and Newfoundland.

The Asiento Treaty

5. By a separate treaty Spain granted Britain the right of supplying the Spanish colonies with black slaves. This was known as the Asiento Treaty, from the Spanish *asiento* (contract) *de negros*. She also allowed one British ship per year to trade in commodities, other than slaves, with Cartagena or Portobello on the Spanish Main.

What did these peace terms mean for the major powers of Europe? The main object for which the Emperor had officially entered the war – to prevent the Bourbon Succession in Spain – was not achieved; on the other hand, the Austrian Habsburgs had concentrated their military efforts in more accessible Italy and they ended the war as the premier power there. The main object of Spain was not achieved either: they did not preserve an undivided Spanish Empire, but they did keep their American possessions and remained a significant power in the Atlantic and Mediterranean. The Dutch had achieved their objective, to check the power of France, but the huge effort involved was a partial cause of their gradual eclipse as a leading naval and commercial power. Britain, on the other hand, had not only checked the might of Louis XIV, but had taken over from the Dutch as the principal naval power. As for France, it had suffered a serious reverse, but it had managed to keep many of the chief gains of Louis XIV, such as Alsace in the east and a much strengthened border with the Netherlands in the north. Given France's agricultural wealth and large population, it would continue to be the foremost land power in 18th century Europe.

Before they had finished making peace with France and Spain, the Tories turned, with no less willingness and considerably greater zest, to attack their enemies at home. Sir Robert Walpole, a young Whig member of the last ministry, and a future Prime Minister of Great Britain, was sent to the Tower on a charge of corruption (1712). Godolphin was dying, but such were the attacks in Parliament against Marlborough that the great general, who earlier had been rewarded with the land and money required to build the huge Blenheim Palace in Oxfordshire, had to flee to the Netherlands and Germany, where he remained until the death of the Queen and the fall of the Tories. So far could party malice lead Englishmen in the days of Queen Anne. The Tories also began an attack on the Dissenters, who were Whig supporters. A Schism Act, reminiscent of the English acts against the Irish, was passed through Parliament, by which the secondary schools kept by Dissenters were to be suppressed.[32]

The Tories attack their enemies

Schism Act 1714

The failing health of the Queen made the situation of the Tory ministry precarious. The Whigs were already in communication with Georg Ludwig, Elector of Hanover, whose aged mother, the Dowager Electress Sophia, was Anne's heiress under the Act of Settlement. The Tory ministers, on the other hand, were not loved in Hanover thanks to their failure to support the British allies, which included Hanover, in the final phase of the war against France. The Earl of Oxford could not make up his mind to prepare for the Queen's death by urgently repairing relations with the Elector George. He was distracted by divisions within his party and especially by the scheming

---

[32] The schism Act was a dead letter: actually only two or three schools were closed. It remained on the Statute Book for five years.

Bolingbroke
in power July
1714
of Bolingbroke, whose main concern was to get rid of him. Anne finally dismissed Oxford on July 27th 1714. Bolingbroke, however, had no time to consolidate himself in power, for on August 1st Queen Anne died. Bolingbroke's enemies declared that he meant to restore the elder line of Stuarts in the person of 'James III', known to history as the Old Pretender, but in fact given the Pretender's refusal to declare himself a Protestant, Bolingbroke seems to have concluded by the spring of 1714 that there was no politically feasible alternative to the succession of the Elector of Hanover.

Death of
Anne
Aug. 1714

The Electress Sophia had died just before the Queen, and Bolingbroke joined the Whigs in proclaiming the Elector as George I of England. The new King landed in England in September; his first action was to dismiss Bolingbroke and install the Whigs in power. Bolingbroke fled to France and joined the Pretender. The Whigs and Tories had struggled for power between 1688 and 1714; but now the Whigs were able to claim that they, and they alone, were the true upholders of the Revolution settlement. The Tories proved too divided and poorly led effectively to dispute the Whig claim. Proceeding with skill and ruthlessness, the Whigs established themselves in power for half a century.

Accession of
George 1714

Conclusion

Between 1603 and 1714 Britain's power and importance in the world had been transformed. When Queen Elizabeth died, Britain lacked the ability to intervene effectively on the continent of Europe, but in 1704 an English general defeated the French and in 1713 Britain, together with France, was the chief architect of the Peace of Utrecht. This access of power depended on Britain's increased wealth, but also on the government's ability to tap it, which developed once the monarch and Parliament at last worked out a way of co-operating, in the last quarter century of Stuart rule. The British had certainly not solved all their problems by 1714. The new Hanoverian dynasty inspired little affection. The Union with Scotland was a fragile creation, based less on mutual affection than on the fear that without Union there would be war. Ireland, crushed but resentful, could become an Achilles heel in future conflicts. Hostility between Anglicans and Dissenters was at the root of the party conflict that threatened at times to tear English society apart. Nonetheless, if these problems proved surmountable, Britain looked likely to play a major role in European politics and to develop its influence and power in the world outside Europe. In both areas, its principal rival was certain to be France. The century after Queen Anne's death, 1714 to 1815, was to be dominated by a titanic struggle between Britain and France for which the wars of William and Anne had been only a curtain-raiser.

Date Summary: William and Mary and Anne (1688-1714)

INDEX

INDEX

INDEX

INDEX